PYTHON

PROGRAMMING

Learn Python in a Week
and Master it

---

7 Days Crash Course

An hands-on introduction to computer programming and algorithms, a project-based guide with practical exercises (BOOK 1)

Computer Programming Academy

Table of Contents

Introduction

Congratulations on purchasing *Python programming: An hands-on introduction to computer programming and algorithms, a project-based guide with practical exercises (Book 1)*, and thank you for doing so.

The following chapters will discuss various fundamental concepts of the Python programming language. There are 7 chapters in this book, crafted specifically to help you master basic and advanced python programming concepts required to develop web based programs and applications in just a week.

The first chapter of this book starts with an introduction to computer programming and some of the most widely used programming languages. You will also learn the fundamental elements of computer programming language such as basic operators, functions, decision making, among others. The importance of mathematical concepts such as algebra and statistics in computer programming has also been explained. Chapter 2 will provide a detailed overview of Python and its historical development. Step by step instructions to install Python on your operating systems have also been included. The concept of Python comments, variables and data types that serve as a prerequisite to the learning of Python programming have been explained in detail.

Chapter 3 is a detailed overview of the basic concepts of Python programming focusing on various programming elements such as Booleans, Tuples, Sets, Dictionaries and much more. The nuances of how to write efficient and effective Python codes have been explained in detail along with plenty of examples and sample exercises to help you solidify your understanding of these concepts. Chapter 4 pertains to the advance Python programming concepts that are relatively more complicated and require a solid understanding of the basic concepts. You will learn how to use OOPS concepts, different loops and conditional statements to generate sophisticated commands. This chapter also includes plenty of examples and sample exercises so you can verify what you have learned.

Like most programming languages, Python boasts a number of built-in functions to make your life easier while coding a software program. Chapter 5 contains a list of all such built-in functions, methods and keywords that can be used to easily develop and run advance codes. Chapter 6 will provide a detailed overview of Django which is web framework that is popularly used in the development of web based programs and applications. You will learn how to install Django on your computer and follow the step by step coding instructions to develop your own web based program and notes taking application.

The final chapter, "Python Applications", will provide details on how Python programming is being used in the development and testing of software programs, machine learning algorithms and Artificial Intelligence technologies to solve real world problems. These cutting edge technologies have resulted in tools and programs that are being utilized across the industrial spectrum to solve real world problems and become more futuristic. This chapter also includes various Python programming tips and tricks that will help you take your coding skills to the next level.

Day 1: Computer Programming 101

Humans have evolved their medium of communication over centuries, resulting in a wide variety of languages spoken across the world. However, all manmade languages have a shared set of features that are remarkably standard across the board. Every language has a script containing different parts of a structured sentence such as nouns, verbs, adjectives, and other elements.

This is where we can draw a bridge to the computer programming languages, which are also composed of a variety of fundamental elements. We will look at each of these elements in detail later in this chapter. However, computer languages allow humans to interact with and guide the computing machines to perform desired operations. It allows the development and implementation of advance computing technologies. These programming languages also allow computers to interact with one another.

Here is a quick overview of some of the most popular computer programming languages.

C

C Language can be defined as a structure-oriented (functions are stored as a self-contained unit), medium level programming language widely utilized in the development of "low-level" applications (pertaining to hardware components of the computer). In 1972, Bell Laboratories developed the C language for implementation in the UNIX system. A number of sophisticated and advanced programming languages such as Java, JavaScript, C++, C# and Perl are derived from the "grandmother" C language. Until the introduction of Java, the C language was the most dominant high-level language of the industry. Some of the only operating systems like IBM System/370 were also developed using the C language.

The C language is rated low on the scale of learning difficulty primarily owing to the limited number of keywords,32, that need to be trained on, and thus, it often serves as a foundational language for coding beginners. It is often used for the development of software applications that require integration to an operating system like UNIX, Linux and Windows. Some of the most popular C language based applications are: Word processors, OS development, database systems, network drivers and interpreters, compilers and assemblers, spreadsheets and graphics packages. Facebook's TAO systems are developed using the C language.

C++

Developed in 1983 as an extension of the C language, C++ can be defined as an object oriented (grouping of function and the associated dataset into an object), "medium level" (interacting with the programming layer of the computer) programming language that can be used for the development of general purpose software. It allows coding in similar syntax as the C language making C++ a perfect example of a "hybrid language". The C++ language with a robust standard library and (STL) quick processing and compilation mechanism, is used to develop various application suites such as "Microsoft Office", graphics editing tools, video editors, gaming packages and even entire Operating Systems. The

"BlackBerry" operating system and the latest Microsoft Office suite are developed entirely on the C++ language.

The C++ language is widely perceived as the enhanced version of the C language with object oriented up to approach that can be used to generate efficient and lean code. It also provides a high level of abstraction to allow improved management of large development projects. The C++ language tends to be the first programming language taught at college level. Some of the major companies and organizations using C++ are Amazon, Google, Adobe software, Mozilla, Winamp, and Lockheed Martin. The C++ language is specifically used in the development of Embedded Firmware, Client Server Applications, Drivers, and system programs.

C#

In 2000, Microsoft released C# (pronounced as C-sharp) as part of its .Net framework, which was developed using other languages like C, C++, and Java as a foundational basis. In 2003, C# became an ISO certified multi-paradigm programming language with powerful features including high functionality, object oriented, imperativeness, declarative attributes and component orientation. Developers use C# a lot to write codes for the XML web services applications as well as Applications connected with Microsoft .Net for the Windows Operating System. The C# language is the go to programming language for Microsoft applications and the language of choice for the Windows Presentation Foundation (WPF). With the introduction of .Net Standard and .Net Core, the .Net ecosystem evolved into cross-platform frameworks and standards, capable of running on Windows, Linux and Mac. The C# language is ideal for beginners and has similar capabilities as Java. It is a high level programming language with high similarity to the English language reading, making it easy to learn and use. It is still not as high level and easy to learn for beginners as Python. Game development is another population application for the C# language, said to be the language of choice to develop and enhance games on the "Unity Game Engine". Developers can write android and iOS applications in C# using Microsoft Xamarin framework.

Java

Java, now owned by Oracle, was introduced in 1991 by Sun Microsystems as a high-level, memory managed language called "Oak" to add capabilities to the C++ language. It is the leading development language and framework with features like general-purpose, object-oriented making it ideal for web based application development. Java runs on the principle of WORA (Write Once Run Anywhere) and has cross-platform capability, making it ideal for developing mobile and gaming applications at the enterprise level.

The Java Server Pages (JSP) is used to develop web based applications. Java allows applications to be accessed through a browser and easily downloadable. The Java byte code is compiled from the Java language and runs on the Java Virtual Machine (JVM). These JVMs are available for a majority of operating systems like Windows and Mac. Some programs that are developed using Java are Eclipse, Lotus Notes, Minecraft, Adobe Creative Suite and open office. Google's Android operating system and app development are primarily driven by Java. It is a robust and interpreted language with high application portability, extensive network library and automatic memory management.

JavaScript

Due to a similarity in the name, people often assume that there is an underlying connection to Java, but it's far from the truth. JavaScript was developed in 1995 by the company Netscape and called "LiveScript". JavaScript processes commands on the computer instead of a server and runs inside a client browser. It is primarily used in web development to make webpages more dynamic and manipulate various elements such as: creating a calendar functionality, printing time and date, adding webpage scrolling abilities and other features that cannot be developed using plain HTML.

Web server called NodeJS runs entirely on JavaScript on the server-side. JavaScript is frequently used by front-end web developers and game developers in a variety of domains such as marketing, information technology, engineering, healthcare and finance. A British agency called Cyber-Duck was developed with JavaScript and uses public APIs to access data concerning crime and enable authorities to review and safeguard local areas. Pete Smart and Robert Hawkes created "Tweetmap", that serves as a depiction of the world map in proportion to the number of "tweets" generated by each country. The fundamental features of JavaScript are considered relatively easy to understand and master. A comprehensive JavaScript library called "JQuery" containing multiple frameworks is widely used by the developers as reference.

Python

Python first introduced in 1989 and is touted as extremely user-friendly and easy to learn programming language for amateurs and entry level coders. It is considered perfect for people who have newly taken up interest in programming or coding and need to understand the fundamentals of programming. This emanates from the fact that Python reads almost like English language. Therefore, it requires less time to understand how the language works and focus can be directed in learning the basics of programming.

Here are some of the fundamental elements of computer programming language:

- **Data Type** – This concept is applicable to every programming language ever designed. The data type is simply a representation of the type of

11

data that needs to be processed by the computer. Some of the most common data types are string, numeric, alphanumeric, decimals, among others. Each programming language has its own definition of the data types and keywords used to write the code. For example, the keyword "char" is used to define string data type in C and Java.

- **Variable** – Data values can be stored on a computer by specifying desired label or name to select computer memory locations. These labels are referred to as variables. For instance, you can store values like "Christmas is on" and "12/25" using variables like "A" and "B" and then subsequently execute scientific program to retrieve desired output. Every programming language will have unique keywords and syntax to create and use required variables.

- **Keywords** – Each programming language has a basic syntax with certain words reserved to indicate specific meaning and cannot be used to create variable names. For example, C programming language used words like "int" and

12

"float" to indicate data types; therefore, you will not be able to create variables named "int" or "float".

- **Basic Operators** – Programming language operators refer to symbols that inform the program compiler to perform the indicated mathematical, logical or relational operation and produce desired output. For example, the arithmetic operator "+" in C programming language will execute the addition command on indicated values. Similarly, relational operator ">" will allow you to compare data values and generate true or false result.

- **Decision Making** – This element pertains to selection of one of the provided options on the basis of the provided conditions. For instance, if a remark needs to be printed, the programming code needs to include one or more required conditional statements that will be processed through the workflow of the program. "If" and "If else" conditional statements are some of the decision making statements used in C and Python.

- **Functions** – A set of reusable and organized code that can be utilized to execute a related action is called as function. They offer enhanced modularity for the app and more reusability of the code. For instance, built in functions like "main ()" or "printf ()" can be written and used in C programming language. Different languages refer to functions using different terminologies like subroutine, method, or procedure.

- **File I/O** – Data values can be stored in various formats such as images, plain texts, rich media, and more using computer files. You can organize these files into distinct directories. In short, files hold data and directories hold files. For instance , the extension ".c" will be added to the end of C programming files and extension ".java" to all Java files. The input files can be created in text editing tools like MS Word or Notepad and output files allows reading of the data from the file. The output files are used to show the results on the screen by executing the input to the program from the command prompt.

Importance of Mathematics in Computer Programming

The discipline of mathematics is extremely important to learn and understand the fundamental concepts of computer programming. Various concepts of "Discrete Mathematics", such as probability, algebra, set theory, logic notation, among others, are intricate parts of computer programming. Algebra is frequently used in programming languages. For example, "Boolean Algebra" can be utilized in logical operations and "Relational Algebra" can be utilized in databases. Another example is used of "Number Theory" in the development of cryptocurrency.

Computer science algorithms, including machine learning algorithms, consist of a set of instructions required in the implementation of an application or program. A basic algorithm is as simple as a mathematics statement written using logical operator "+" (5+7 = 12) to code for the addition of data values. The whole concept of data analysis and problem solving is dependent on the mathematical equations that are analyzed to understand the crux of an error. By addressing those issues directly using the mathematics of the program, hard fixes can be easily made to the application.

Statistics is also widely used in data mining and compression, as well as speech recognition and image analysis software. The field of Artificial Intelligence and Machine Learning share a lot of core concepts from the field of statistics. "Statistical learning" is a descriptive statistics-based learning framework that can be categorized as supervised or unsupervised. "Supervised statistical learning" includes constructing a statistical model to predict or estimate output based on single or multiple inputs, on the other hand, "unsupervised statistical learning" involves inputs but no supervisory output, but helps in learning data relationships and structure. One way of understanding statistical learning is to identify the connection between the "predictor" (autonomous variables, attributes) and the "response" (autonomous variable), in order to produce a specific model which is capable of predicting the "response variable (Y)" on the basis of "predictor factors (X)".

"*X = f(X) + ε where X = (X1,X2, . . .,Xp)*", where "f" is an "*unknown function*" & "*ε*" is "*random error (reducible & irreducible)*".

If there are a number of inputs "X" easily accessible, but the output "B" production is unknown, "f" is often treated as a black box, provided that it generates accurate predictions for "Y". This is called "prediction". There are circumstances in which we need to understand how "Y" is influenced as "X" changes. We want to estimate "f" in this scenario, but our objective is not simply to generate predictions for "Y". In this situation, we want to establish and better understand the connection between "Y" and "X". Now "f" is not regarded as a black box since we have to understand the underlying process of the system. This is called "inference". In everyday life, various issues can be categorized into the setting of "predictions", the setting of "inferences", or a "hybrid" of the two.

The "parametric technique" can be defined as an evaluation of "f" by calculating the set parameters (finite summary of the data) while establishing an assumption about the functional form of "f". The mathematical equation of this technique is "$f(X) = \beta 0 + \beta 1 X 1 + \beta 2 X 2 + \ldots + \beta p X p$". The "parametric models" tend to have a finite number of parameters which is independent of the size of the data set. This is also known as "model-based learning". For example, "k-Gaussian models" are driven by parametric techniques.

On the other hand, the "non-parametric technique" generates an estimation of "f" on the basis of its closeness to the data points, without making any assumptions on the functional form of "f". The "non-parametric models" tend to have a varying number of parameters, which grows proportionally with the size of the data set. This is also known as "memory-based learning". For example, "kernel density models" are driven by a non-parametric technique.

Day 2: Introduction to Python

Python is a high-level programming language, commonly used for general purposes. It was originally developed by Guido van Rossum at the "Center Wiskunde & Informatica (CWI), Netherlands", in the 1980s and introduced by the "Python Software Foundation" in 1991. It was designed primarily to emphasize the readability of programming code, and its syntax enables programmers to convey ideas using fewer lines of code. Python programming language increases the speed of operation while allowing for higher efficiency in creating system integrations. Developers are using Python for "web development (server-side), software development, mathematics, system scripting".

With the introduction of various enhancements such as "list comprehension" and a "garbage collection system", which can collect reference cycles, the Python 2.0 was launched in the last quarter of 2000. Subsequently, in 2008, Python 3.0 was released as a major version upgrade with backward compatibility allowing for the Python 2.0 code to be executed on Python 3.0 without requiring any modifications. Python is supported by a community of programmers that continually develop and maintain the "CPython", which is an open-source reference implementation. The "Python Software Foundation" is a not for profit organization that is responsible for managing and directing resources for developing Python programming as well as "CPython".

Here are some of the key features of Python that render it as the language of choice for coding beginners as well as advanced software programmers alike:

1. **Readability**: Python reads a lot like the English language, which contributes to its ease of readability.

2. **Learnability**: Python is a high level programming language and considered easy to learn due to the ability to code using English language like expressions, which implies it is simple to comprehend and thereby learn the language.

3. **Operating Systems**: Python is easily accessible and can be operated across different Operating systems, including Linux, Unix, Mac, Windows among others. This renders Python as a versatile and cross-platform language.

4. **Open Source**: Python is "open source", which means that the developer community can seamlessly make updates to the code, which are always available to anyone using Python for their software programming needs.

5. **Standardized Data Libraries**: Python features a big standard data library with a variety of useful codes and functionalities that can be used when writing Python code for data analysis and development of machine learning models. (Details on machine learning libraries will be provided later in this chapter)

6. **Free**: Considering the wide applicability and usage of Python, it is hard to believe that it continues to be freely available for easy download and use. This implies that anyone looking to learn or use Python can simply download and use it for their applications completely free of charge. Python is indeed a perfect example of a "FLOSS (Free/Libre Open Source Software)", which means one could "freely distribute copies of this software, read its source code and modify it".

7. **Supports managing of exceptions**: An "exception" can be defined as "an event that can

occur during program exception and can disrupt the normal flow of program". Python is capable of supporting handling of these "exceptions", implying that you could write fewer error-prone codes and test your code with a variety of cases, which could potentially lead to an "exception" in the future.

8. **Advanced Features**: Python can also support "generators and list comprehensions".

Storage governance: Python is also able to support "automatic memory management", which implies that the storage memory will be cleared and made available automatically. You are not required to clear and free up the system memory.

Installation Instructions for Python

You can follow the step by step instructions to download and install Python on a variety of operating systems. Simply jump to the section for the operating system you are working on. The latest version of Python released in the middle of the 2019 is Python 3.8.0. Make sure you are downloading and installing the most recent and stable version of Python and following the instructions below.

WINDOWS

1. From the official Python website, click on the "Downloads" icon and select Windows.

2. Click on the "Download Python 3.8.0" button to view all the downloadable files.

3. You will be taken to a different screen where you can select the Python version you would like to download. In this book, we will be using the Python 3 version under "Stable Releases". So scroll down the page and click on the "Download Windows x86-64 executable installer" link, as shown in the picture below.

- Python 3.8.0 - Oct. 14, 2019

  Note that Python 3.8.0 *cannot* be used on Windows XP or earlier.

  - Download Windows help file
  - Download Windows x86-64 embeddable zip file
  - Download Windows x86-64 executable installer
  - Download Windows x86-64 web-based installer
  - Download Windows x86 embeddable zip file
  - Download Windows x86 executable installer
  - Download Windows x86 web-based installer

4. A pop-up window titled "python-3.8.0-amd64.exe" will be displayed.

5. Click on the "Save File" button to start downloading the file.

6. Once the download has completed, double click the saved file icon, and a "Python 3.8.0 (64-bit) Setup" pop window will be displayed.

7. Make sure that you select the "Install Launcher for all users (recommended)" and the "Add Python 3.8 to PATH" checkboxes. Note – If you already have an older version of Python installed on your system, the "Upgrade Now" button will appear instead of the "Install Now" button, and neither of the checkboxes will be displayed.

8. Click on the "Install Now" button and a "User Account Control" pop up window will be displayed.

9. A notification stating, "Do you want to allow this app to make change to your device" will be displayed, click on Yes.

10. A new pop up window titled "Python 3.8.0 (64-bit) Setup" will be displayed containing a setup progress bar.

11. Once the installation has been completed, a "Set was successful" message will be displayed. Click on the Close button, and you are all set.

12. To verify the installation, navigate to the directory where you installed Python and double click on the python.exe file.

MACINTOSH

1. From the official Python website, click on the "Downloads" icon and select Mac.

2. Click on the "Download Python 3.8.0" button to view all the downloadable files.

3. You will be taken to a different screen where you can select the Python version you would like to download. In this book, we will be using the Python 3 version under "Stable Releases". So scroll down the page and click on the "Download macOS 64-bit installer" link under Python 3.8.0, as shown in the picture below.

- Python 3.7.5 - Oct. 15, 2019
  - Download macOS 64-bit/32-bit installer
  - Download macOS 64-bit installer
- Python 3.8.0 - Oct. 14, 2019
  - Download macOS 64-bit installer
- Python 3.7.4 - July 8, 2019
  - Download macOS 64-bit/32-bit installer
  - Download macOS 64-bit installer
- Python 3.6.9 - July 2, 2019

4. A pop-up window titled "python-3.8.0-macosx10.9.pkg" will be displayed.

5. Click on the "Save File" button to start downloading the file.

6. Once the download has completed, double click the saved file icon, and an "Install Python" pop window will be displayed.

7. Click on the "Continue" button to proceed, and a terms and conditions pop up window will be displayed.

8. Click Agree and then click on the "Install" button.

9. A notification requesting administrator permission and password will be displayed. Simply enter your system password to begin installation.

10. Once the installation has been completed, an "Installation was successful" message will be displayed. Click on the Close button, and you are all set.

11. To verify the installation, navigate to the directory where you installed Python and double click on the python launcher icon that will take you to the Python Terminal.

LINUX

- **For Red Hat, CentOS, or Fedora**, install the python3 and python3-devel packages.
- **For Debian or Ubuntu**, install the python3.x and python3.x-dev packages.
- **For Gentoo**, install the '=python-3.x*' ebuild (you may have to unmask it first).

1. From the official Python website, click on the "Downloads" icon and select Linux/UNIX.

2. Click on the "Download Python 3.8.0" button to view all the downloadable files.

3. You will be taken to a different screen where you can select the Python version you would like to download. In this book, we will be using the Python 3 version under "Stable Releases". So scroll down the page and click on the "Download Gzipped source tarball" link under Python 3.8.0, as shown in the picture below.

- Download Gzipped source tarball

- Download XZ compressed source tarball

- Python 3.8.0 - Oct. 14, 2019

  - Download Gzipped source tarball

  - Download XZ compressed source tarball

- Python 3.7.4 - July 8, 2019

  - Download Gzipped source tarball

  - Download XZ compressed source tarball

4.   A pop-up window titled "python-3.7.5.tgz" will be displayed.

5.   Click on the "Save File" button to start downloading the file.

6.   Once the download has completed, double click the saved file icon, and an "Install Python" pop window will be displayed.

7.   Follow the prompts on the screen to complete the installation process.

Getting Started

Now that you have the Python terminal installed on your computer, we will now see how you can start writing and executing the Python code. All Python codes are written in a text editor as (.py) files, which are then executed on the Python interpreter on the command line as shown in the code below, where "smallworld.py" is the name of the Python file:

"C: \Users\Your Name\python smallworld.py"

You can test a small code without writing the code in a file and simply executing it as a command-line itself by typing the code below on the Mac, Windows or Linux command line, as shown below:

"C: \Users\Your Name\python"

In case the above command doesn't work, you can use the code below instead

"C: \Users\Your Name\py"

Indentation – To understand the Python coding structure, you must first understand the significance of indentation or the number of spaces before you start typing the code. Unlike other coding languages where "indentation" is added to enhance the readability of the code, in Python, it is used to indicate a set of code. For example, look at the code below

If 7 > 4:

print ('Seven is greater than 4')

There is indentation prior to the second line of code with the print command. If you skip the indentation and write the code as below, you will receive an error:

If 7 > 4:

print ('Seven is greater than 4')

The number of spaces can be adjusted but must be at least single-spaced. For example, you can execute the code below with higher indentation, but for a specific set of code same number of spaces must be used, or you will receive an error.

If 7 > 4:

print ('Seven is greater than 4')

Adding Comments – In Python, you can add comments to the code by starting the code comment lines with a "#", as shown in the example below:

#Add any relevant comment here

print ('Planet Earth')

Comments are also used as a description of the code and not executed by the Python terminal. It is important to remember that if you put a comment at the end of code like the entire code line will be skipped by the Python terminal, as shown in the code below. Comments are extremely useful in case you need to stop the execution when you are testing the code.

print ('Planet Earth') #Add comments here

You can also add multiple lines of comments by starting each code line with "#", as shown below:

#Add comment here
#Supplement the comment here
#Further add the comment here
print ('Planet Earth')

Python Variables

In Python, variables are used to store data values without executing a command for it. You can create a variable by simply assigning desired value to it, as shown in the example below:

A = 110
B = 'David'

print (A)

print (B)

A variable may be declared without a specific data type. The data type of a variable can also be modified after its initial declaration, as shown in the example below:

A = 110 # A has data type set as int

A = 'David' # A now has data type str

print (A)

There are certain rules applied to the Python variable names as follows:

1. Variable names can be short as single alphabets or more descriptive words like height, weight, etc

2. Variable names can only be started with an underscore character or a letter.

3. Variable names must not start with numbers.

4. Variable names may contain underscores or alphanumeric characters. No other special characters are allowed.

5. Variable names are case sensitive. For example, 'height,' 'Height' and 'HEIGHT' will be accounted as 3 separate variables.

Assigning Value to Variables

In Python, multiple variables can be assigned DISTINCT values in a single code line, as shown in the example below:

A, B, C = 'lilac,' 'red,' 'cyan'

print (A)

print (B)

print (C)

OR multiple variables can be assigned SAME value in a single code line, as shown in the example below:

A, B, C = 'lilac'

print (A)

print (B)

print (C)

Python Data Types

To further understand the concept of variables, let's first look at the Python data types. Python supports a variety of data types as listed below:

Category	Data Type	Example Syntax
Text	*"str"*	'Planet Earth' "Planet Earth" """Planet Earth"""
Boolean	*"bool"*	'True' 'False'
Mapping (mixed data types, associative array of key and value pairs)	*"dict"*	'{'key9' : 9.0, 6 : True}'
Sequence (may contain mixed data types)	*"list"*	'[9.0, 'character', True]'
	"tuple"	'[9.0, 'character,' True]'
	"range"	'range (10, 50)' 'range (100, 50, 10,-10,-50,-100)'
Binary	*"bytes"*	b 'byte

		sequence' b `byte sequence' bytes ([120, 90, 75, 100])
	"bytearray"	bytearray (b `byte sequence') bytearray (b `byte sequence') bytearray ([120, 90, 75, 100])
	"memoryview"	
Set (unordered, no duplicates, mixed data types)	*"set"*	`[9.0, `character,' True]'
	"frozenset"	`frozenset ([9.0, `character', True])'
Numeric	*"int"*	`54'
	"float"	`18e9'
	"complex"	`18 + 3.1j'

Ellipsis (index in NumPy arrays)	*"ellipsis"*	`'...'` 'Ellipsis'

To view the data type of any object, you can use the *"type ()"* function as shown in the example below:

A = 'Lilac'

print (type (A))

Assigning the Data Type to Variables

As mentioned earlier, you can create a new variable by simply declaring a value for it. This set data value, in turn, assigns the data type to the variable.

To assign a specific data type to a variable, the constructor functions listed below can be used:

Constructor Functions	Data Type
A = str ('Planet Earth)'	str
A = int (99)	Int (Must be a whole number, positive or negative with no decimals, no length restrictions)
A = float (15e6)	Float (Floating point number must be a positive or

	negative number with one or more decimals; maybe scientific number an 'e' to specify an exponential power of 10)
A = complex (99j)	Complex (Must be written with a 'j' as an imaginary character)
A = list (('cyan', 'red', 'olive'))	list
A = range (1, 100)	range
A = tuple (('cyan', 'red', 'olive'))	tuple
A = set (('cyan', 'red', 'olive'))	set
A = frozenset (('cyan', 'olive', 'red'))	frozenset
A = dict ('color' : 'red', 'year' : 1999)	dict
A = bool (False)	bool
A = bytes (54)	bytes
A = bytearray (8)	bytearray
A = memoryview (bytes (55))	memoryview

EXERCISE – To solidify your understanding of data types. Look at the first column of the table below and write the data type for that variable. Once you have all your answers, look at the second column, and verify your answers.

Variable	Data Type
A = 'Planet Earth'	str
A = 99	int
A = 29e2	float
A = 99j	complex
A = ['cyan', 'red,' 'olive']	list
A = range (1, 100)	range
A = ('cyan,' 'red,' 'olive')	tuple
A = {'cyan', 'red', 'olive'}	set
A = frozenset ({ 'cyan', 'olive', 'red'})	frozenset
A = ['color' : 'red', 'year' : 1999}	dict
A = False	bool
A = b 'Welcome'	bytes
A = bytearray (8)	bytearray
A = memoryview (bytes (55))	memoryview

Output Variables

In order to retrieve variables as output, the "print" statements are used in Python. You can use the "+"

character to combine text with a variable for final output, as shown in the example below:

'A = 'red'

print ('Apples are' + A)'

OUTPUT – 'Apples are red'

A variable can also be combined with another variable using the "+" character, as shown in the example below:

'A = 'Apples are'

B = 'red'

AB = A + B

print (AB)'

OUTPUT – 'Apples are red'

However, when the "+" character is used with numeric values, it retains its function as a mathematical operator, as shown in the example below:

'A = 20

B = 30

print (A + B)'

OUTPUT = 50

You will not be able to combine a string of characters with numbers and will trigger an error instead, as shown in the example below:

A = 'red'

B = 30

print (A + B)

OUTPUT – N/A – ERROR

Day 3: Coding Basics

In the previous chapter, you learned the basics of Python syntax, the concept of Python Variables, and Comments that serve as a prerequisite to the learning of Python programming. In this chapter, we will be looking at the nuances of how to write efficient and effective Python codes, focusing on various programming elements such as Booleans, Tuples, Sets, Dictionaries and much more. So let's get started.

Python Numbers

In Python programming, you will be working with 3 different numeric data types, namely, "int", "float", and "complex". In the previous chapter, you learned the details of what these data types entail, but below are some examples to refresh your memory.

Data Type	Example
Int (Must be a whole number, positive or negative with no decimals, no length restrictions)	*363 or 3.214*

Float (Floating point number must be a positive or negative number with one or more decimals; maybe scientific number an "e" to specify an exponential power of 10)	*29e3*
Complex (Must be written with a "j" as an imaginary character)	*92j*

EXERCISE – Create variable "a" with data value as "3.24", variable "b" with data value as "9e3" and variable "c" with data value as "-39j".

USE YOUR DISCRETION HERE AND WRITE YOUR CODE FIRST

Now, check your code against the correct code below:

a = 3.24 # int

b = 9e3 # float

c = -39j # complex

print (type (a))

print (type (b))

print (type (c))

Note – The # comments are not required for the correct code and are only mentioned to bolster your understanding of the concept.

Converting one numeric data type to another

As all Python variables are dynamic in nature, you will be able to convert the data type of these variables if needed by deriving a new variable from the variable that you would like to assign a new data type.

Let's continue building on the exercise discussed above.

a = 3.24 # int

b = 9e3 # float

c = -39j # complex

#conversion from int to float

x = float (a)

#conversion from float to complex

y = complex (b)

#conversion from complex to int

z = float (c)

```
#conversion from int to complex
x1 = int (a)

print (x)
print (y)
print (z)
print (x1)

print (type (x))
print (type (y))
print (type (z))
print (type (x1))
```

EXERCISE – View a random number between 14 and 24 by importing the random module.

USE YOUR DISCRETION HERE AND WRITE YOUR CODE FIRST

Now, check your code against the correct code below:
import random

print (random.randrange (14, 24))

Variable Casting with Constructor Functions

In the discussion and exercise above, you learned that variables could be declared by simply assigning desired data value to them, and thereby, the variables will assume the pertinent data type based on the data value. However, Python allows you to specify the data types for variables by using classes or "constructor functions" to define the data type for variables. This process is called "Casting".

Here are the 3 constructor functions used for "casting" numeric data type to a variable.

Constructor Functions	Data Type
int ()	Will construct an integer number from an integer literal, a string literal (provided the string is representing a whole number) or a float literal (by rounding down to the preceding whole number)
float ()	Will construct a float number from a string literal (provided the string is representing a float or an integer), a float literal or an integer literal

complex ()	Will construct a string from a large number of data types, such as integer literals, float literals, and strings

Here are some examples:

Integer:

a = int (6)   *# a takes the value 6*

b = int (4.6)   *# b takes the value 4*

c = int ('7')   *# c takes the value 7*

Float:

a = float (6)   *# a takes the value 6.0*

b = float (4.6) *# b takes the value 4.6*

c = float ('7')   *# c takes the value 7.0*

String:

a = str ('serial')   *# a takes the value 'serial'*

b = str (4.6)   *# b takes the value '4.6'*

c = str ('7')   *# c takes the value '7.0'*

Python Strings

In Python, string data type for a variable is denoted by using single, double, or triple quotation marks. This implies that you can assign string data value to variable by quoting the string of characters. For example, "welcome" is the same as 'welcome' and '"welcome"'.

EXERCISE – Create a variable "v" with a string data value as "outfit is cyan" and display it.

USE YOUR DISCRETION HERE AND WRITE YOUR CODE FIRST

Now, check your code against the correct code below:
v = 'outfit is cyan'
print (v)

OUTPUT – outfit is cyan

EXERCISE – Create a variable "A" with a multiple-line string data value as "Looking at the sky tonight, thinking of you by my side! Let the world go on and on; it will be alright if I stay strong!" and display it.
USE YOUR DISCRETION HERE AND WRITE YOUR CODE FIRST

Now, check your code against the correct code below:

```
a = '''Loving another is never easy,
People tell you it won't be breezy!
You make your own decision,
Don't let the fear stop you from your persuasion!'''
print (a)
```

OUTPUT – Loving another is never easy,

People tell you it won't be breezy!

You make your own decision,

Don't let the fear stop you from your persuasion!'''

Note – You must use triple quote to create multiline string data values.

String Arrays

In Python, string data values are arrays of bytes that represent Unicode characters as true for most programming languages. But unlike other programming languages, Python lacks data type for individual characters, which are denoted as string data type with length of 1.

The first character of every string is given the position of '0', and subsequently, the subsequent characters will have the position as 1, 2, 3, and so on. In order to display desired characters from a string data value, you can use the position of the character enclosed in square brackets. For example, if you wanted to display the fifth character of the string data value "apple" of variable "x". You will use the command "print (x [4])"

EXERCISE – Create a variable "P" with a string data value as "brilliant" and display the fourth character of this string.

USE YOUR DISCRETION HERE AND WRITE YOUR CODE FIRST

Now, check your code against the correct code below:

P = 'brilliant'
print (P [4])

OUTPUT – l

Slicing

If you would like to view a range of characters, you can do so by specifying the start and the end index of the desired positions and separating the indexes by a colon.

For example, to view characters of a string from position 1 to position 3, your code will be *"print (variable [1:3])"*.

You can even view the characters starting from the end of the string by using "negative indexes" and start slicing the string from the end of the string. For example, to view characters of a string from position 4 to position 1, your code will be *"print (variable [-4 : -2])"*.

In order to view the length of the string, you can use the "len ()" function. For example, to view the length of a string, your code will be *"print (len (variable))"*.

EXERCISE – Create a variable "P" with a string data value as "strive for success!" and display characters from position 3 to 6 of this string.

USE YOUR DISCRETION HERE AND WRITE YOUR CODE FIRST

Now, check your code against the correct code below:
P = 'strive for success!'
print (P [4 : 7])

OUTPUT – vef

EXERCISE – Create a variable "x" with a string data value as "coding is cool" and display characters from position 6 to 1, starting the count from the end of this string.

USE YOUR DISCRETION HERE AND WRITE YOUR CODE FIRST

Now, check your code against the correct code below:
x = 'coding is cool'
print (x [-6 : -2])

OUTPUT - isco

EXERCISE – Create a variable "z" with a string data value as "programming champ" and display the length of this string.

USE YOUR DISCRETION HERE AND WRITE YOUR CODE FIRST

Now, check your code against the correct code below:

```
z = 'programming champ'
print (len (z))
```

OUTPUT - 16

String Methods

There are various built-in methods in Python that can be applied to string data values. Here are the Python codes for some of the most frequently used string methods, using variable "P = 'roses are red!'".

"strip ()" method – To remove any blank spaces at the start and the end of the string.

```
P = "    roses are red!    "
print (P.strip ())
```

OUTPUT – roses are red!

"lower ()" method – To result in all the characters of a string in lower case.

```
P = "ROSES are RED!"
print (P.lower ())
```

52

OUTPUT – roses are red!

"upper ()" method – To result in all the characters of a string in upper case.

P = "Roses are Red!"
print (P.upper ())

OUTPUT – ROSES ARE RED!

"replace ()" method – To replace select characters of a string.

P = "roses are red!"
print (P.replace ("roses", "apples"))

OUTPUT – apples are red!

"split ()" method – To split a string into substrings using comma as the separator.

P = "Roses, Apples"
print (P.split ("",))

OUTPUT – ['Roses',   'Apples']

String Concatenation

There might be instances when you need to collate different string variables. This can be accomplished with the use of the "+" logical operator. Here's the syntax for this Python code:

X = "string1"

Y = "string2"

Z = X + Y

print (Z)

Similarly, below is the syntax to insert a blank space between two different string variables.

X = "string1"

Y = "string2"

Z = X + " " + Y

print (Z)

However, Python does not permit the concatenation of string variables with numeric variables. But can be accomplished with the use of the *"format ()"* method, which will format the executed arguments and place them in the string where the placeholders "{ }" are used. Here's the syntax for this Python code:

```
X = numeric
Y = "String"
print (Y. format (X))
```

EXERCISE – Create two variables "A" and "B" with string data values as "Let's have" and "some pizza!" and display them as a concatenated string.

USE YOUR DISCRETION HERE AND WRITE YOUR CODE FIRST

Now, check your code against the correct code below:
```
A = "Let's have"
B = "some pizza!"
C = A + B
print (C)
```

OUTPUT – Let's have some pizza!

EXERCISE – Create two variables "A" with string data values as "her lucky number is" and "B" with numeric data value as "18" and display them as a concatenated string.

*** USE YOUR DISCRETION HERE AND WRITE YOUR CODE FIRST***

Now, check your code against the correct code below:

A = "her lucky number is"

B = "18"

print (A. format (B))

OUTPUT – her lucky number is 18

Python Booleans

In the process of developing a software program, there is often a need to confirm and verify whether an expression is true or false. This is where Python Boolean data type and data values are used. In Python, comparison and evaluation of two data values will result in one of the two Boolean values: "True" or "False".

Here are some examples of comparison statement of numeric data leading to Boolean value:

print (100 > 90)

OUTPUT – True

print (100 == 90)

OUTPUT – False

print (100 < 90)

OUTPUT – False

Let's look at the *"bool ()"* function now, which allows for the evaluation of numeric data as well as string data resulting in "True" or "False" Boolean values.

print (bool (99))

OUTPUT - True

print (bool ("Welcome"))

OUTPUT - True

Here are some key points to remember for Booleans:

1. If a statement has some kind of content, it would be evaluated as "True".

2. All string data values will be resulting as "True" unless the string is empty.

3. All numeric values will be resulting as "True" except "0"

4. Lists, Tuples, Set, and Dictionaries will be resulting as "True" unless they are empty.

5. Mostly empty values like (), [], {}, "", False, None and 0 will be resulting as "False".

6. Any object created with the "_len_" function that result in the data value as "0" or "False" will be evaluated as "False".

In Python there are various built-in functions function that can be evaluated as Boolean, for example, the "isinstance()" function, which allows you to determine the data type of an object. Therefore, in order to check if an object is integer, the code will be as below:

X = 123

print (isinstance (X, int))

EXERCISE – Create two variables "X" with string data values as "Just do it!" and "Y" with numeric data value as "3.24" and evaluate them.

USE YOUR DISCRETION HERE AND WRITE YOUR CODE FIRST

Now, check your code against the correct code below:

X = "Just do it!"

Y = 3.24

print (bool (X))

print (bool (Y)

OUTPUT –

True

True

Python Lists

In Python, lists are collections of data types that can be changed, organized, and include duplicate values. Lists are written within square brackets, as shown in the syntax below.

X = ["string001", "string002", "string003"]
print (X)

The same concept of position applies to Lists as the string data type, which dictates that the first string is considered to be at position 0. Subsequently, the strings that will follow are given positions 1, 2, and so on. You can selectively display desired string from a List by referencing the position of that string inside square bracket in the print command, as shown below.

X = ["string001", "string002", "string003"]
print (X [2])

OUTPUT – [string003]

Similarly, the concept of **negative indexing** is also applied to Python List. Let's look at the example below:

X = ["string001", "string002", "string003"]
print (X [-2])

OUTPUT – [string002]

You will also be able to specify a **range of indexes** by indicating the start and end of a range. The result in values of such command on a Python List would be a new List containing only the indicated items. Here is an example for your reference.

X = ["string001", "string002", "string003", "string004", "string005", "string006"]
print (X [2 : 4])

OUTPUT – ["string003", "string004"]

* Remember the first item is at position 0, and the final position of the range (4) is not included.

Now, if you do not indicate the start of this range, it will default to the position 0 as shown in the example below:
X = ["string001", "string002", "string003", "string004", "string005", "string006"]
print (X [: 3])

OUTPUT – ["string001", "string002", "string003"]

Similarly, if you do not indicate the end of this range it will display all the items of the List from the indicated start range to the end of the List, as shown in the example below:

X = ["string001", "string002", "string003", "string004", "string005", "string006"]
  print (X [3 :])

OUTPUT – ["string004", "string005", "string006"]

You can also specify a **range of negative indexes** to Python Lists, as shown in the example below:
X = ["string001", "string002", "string003", "string004", "string005", "string006"]
  print (X [-3 : -1])

OUTPUT – ["string004", "string005"]

* Remember the last item is at position -1, and the final position of this range (-1) is not included in the Output.

There might be instances when you need to **change the data value** for a Python List. This can be accomplished by referring to the index number of that item and declaring the new value. Let's look at the example below:

X = ["string001", "string002", "string003", "string004", "string005", "string006"]

X [3] = "newstring"

print (X)

OUTPUT – ["string001", "string002", "string003", "newstring", "string005", "string006"]

You can also determine the **length** of a Python List using the "len()" function, as shown in the example below:

X = ["string001", "string002", "string003", "string004", "string005", "string006"]

print (len (X))

OUTPUT – 6

Python Lists can also be changed by **adding new items** to an existing list using the built-in "append ()" method, as shown in the example below:

X = ["string001", "string002", "string003", "string004"]

X.append ("newstring")

print (X)

OUTPUT – ["string001", "string002", "string003", "string004", "newstring"]

You can also, add a new item to an existing Python List at a specific position using the built-in "insert ()" method, as shown in the example below:

X = ["string001", "string002", "string003", "string004"]

X.insert (2, "newstring")

print (X)

OUTPUT – ["string001", "string002", "newstring", "string004"]

There might be instances when you need to **copy** an existing Python List. This can be accomplished by using the built-in "copy ( )" method or the "list ( )" method, as shown in the example below:

X = ["string001", "string002", "string003", "string004", "string005", "string006"]

Y = X.copy( )

print (Y)

OUTPUT – ["string001", "string002", "string003", "string004", "string005", "string006"]

X = ["string001", "string002", "string003", "string004", "string005", "string006"]

Y = list (X)

print (Y)

OUTPUT – ["string001", "string002", "string003", "string004", "string005", "string006"]

There are multiple built-in methods to **delete items** from a Python List.

- To selectively delete a specific item, the "remove ()" method can be used.

X = ["string001", "string002", "string003", "string004"]

X.remove ("string002")

print (X)

OUTPUT - ["string001", "string003", "string004"]

- To delete a specific item from the List, the "pop ()" method can be used with the position of the value. If no index has been indicated, the last item of the index will be removed.

X = ["string001", "string002", "string003", "string004"]
X.pop ( )
print (X)

OUTPUT - ["string001", "string002", "string003"]

- To delete a specific index from the List, the "del ()" method can be used, followed by the index within square brackets.

X = ["string001", "string002", "string003", "string004"]
del X [2]
print (X)

OUTPUT - ["string001", "string002", "string004"]

- To delete the entire List variable, the "del ()" method can be used, as shown below.

X = ["string001", "string002", "string003", "string004"]

del X

OUTPUT - …..

- To delete all the string values from the List without deleting the variable itself, the "clear ()" method can be used, as shown below.

X = ["string001", "string002", "string003", "string004"]

X.clear()

print (X)

OUTPUT – [ ]

Concatenation of Lists

You can join multiple lists with the use of the "+" logical operator or by adding all the items from one list to another using the "append ( )" method. The "extend ( )" method can be used to add a list at the end of another list. Let's look at the examples below to understand these commands.

X = ["string001", "string002", "string003", "string004"]

Y = [10, 20, 30, 40]

Z = X + Y

print (Z)

OUTPUT – ["string001", "string002", "string003", "string004", 10, 20, 30, 40]

X = ["string001", "string002", "string003", "string004"]
Y = [10, 20, 30, 40]

For x in Y:
X.append (x)

print (X)

OUTPUT – ["string001", "string002", "string003", "string004", 10, 20, 30, 40]
X = ["string001", "string002", "string003"]
Y = [10, 20, 30]

X.extend (Y)
print (X)

OUTPUT – ["string001", "string002", "string003", 10, 20, 30]

EXERCISE – Create a list "A" with string data values as "red, olive, cyan, lilac, mustard" and display the item at -2 position.

USE YOUR DISCRETION HERE AND WRITE YOUR CODE FIRST

Now, check your code against the correct code below:
A = ["red", "olive", "cyan", "lilac", "mustard"]
print (A [-2])

OUTPUT – ["lilac"]

EXERCISE – Create a list "A" with string data values as "red, olive, cyan, lilac, mustard" and display the items ranging from the string on the second position to the end of the string.

USE YOUR DISCRETION HERE AND WRITE YOUR CODE FIRST

Now, check your code against the correct code below:
A = ["red", "olive", "cyan", "lilac", "mustard"]
print (A [2 :])

OUTPUT – ["cyan", "lilac", "mustard"]

EXERCISE – Create a list "A" with string data values as "red, olive, cyan, lilac, mustard" and replace the string "olive" to "teal".

USE YOUR DISCRETION HERE AND WRITE YOUR CODE FIRST

Now, check your code against the correct code below:
A = ["red", "olive", "cyan", "lilac", "mustard"]
A [1] = ["teal"]

print (A)

OUTPUT – ["red", "teal", "cyan", "lilac", "mustard"]

EXERCISE – Create a list "A" with string data values as "red, olive, cyan, lilac, mustard" and copy the list "A" to create list "B".

USE YOUR DISCRETION HERE AND WRITE YOUR CODE FIRST

Now, check your code against the correct code below:

A = ["red", "olive", "cyan", "lilac", "mustard"]

B = A.copy ( )

print (B)

OUTPUT – ["red", "olive", "cyan", "lilac", "mustard"]

EXERCISE – Create a list "A" with string data values as "red, olive, cyan, lilac, mustard" and delete the strings "red" and "lilac".

USE YOUR DISCRETION HERE AND WRITE YOUR CODE FIRST

Now, check your code against the correct code below:

A = ["red", "olive", "cyan", "lilac", "mustard"]

del.A [0, 2]

print (A)

OUTPUT – ["olive", "cyan", "mustard"]

Python Tuples

In Python, Tuples are collections of data types that cannot be changed but can be arranged in specific order. Tuples allow for duplicate items and are written within round brackets, as shown in the syntax below.

Tuple = ("string001", "string002", "string003")
print (Tuple)

Similar to the Python List, you can selectively display the desired string from a Tuple by referencing the position of that string inside square bracket in the print command as shown below.

Tuple = ("string001", "string002", "string003")
print (Tuple [1])

OUTPUT – ("string002")

The concept of **negative indexing** can also be applied to Python Tuple, as shown in the example below:

Tuple = ("string001", "string002", "string003", "string004", "string005")
print (Tuple [-2])

OUTPUT – ("string004")

You will also be able to specify a **range of indexes** by indicating the start and end of a range. The result in values of such command on a Python Tuple would be a new Tuple containing only the indicated items, as shown in the example below:

Tuple = ("string001", "string002", "string003", "string004", "string005", "string006")
print (Tuple [1:5])

OUTPUT – *("string002", "string003", "string004", "string005")*

* Remember the first item is at position 0 and the final position of the range, which is the fifth position in this example, is not included.

You can also specify a **range of negative indexes** to Python Tuples, as shown in the example below:
Tuple = ("string001", "string002", "string003", "string004", "string005", "string006")
print (Tuple [-4: -2])

OUTPUT – *("string004", "string005")*

* Remember the last item is at position -1 and the final position of this range, which is the negative fourth position in this example is not included in the Output.

Unlike Python lists, you cannot directly **change the data value of Python Tuples** after they have been created. However, conversion of a Tuple into a List and then modifying the data value of that List will allow you to subsequently create a Tuple from that updated List. Let's look at the example below:

Tuple1 = ("string001", "string002", "string003", "string004", "string005", "string006")

List1 = list (Tuple1)

List1 [2] = "update this list to create new tuple"

Tuple1 = tuple (List1)

print (Tuple1)

OUTPUT – ("string001", "string002", "update this list to create new tuple", "string004", "string005", "string006")

You can also determine the **length** of a Python Tuple using the "len()" function, as shown in the example below:

Tuple = ("string001", "string002", "string003", "string004", "string005", "string006")

print (len (Tuple))

OUTPUT – 6

You cannot selectively delete items from a Tuple, but you can use the "del" keyword to **delete the Tuple** in its entirety, as shown in the example below:

Tuple = ("string001", "string002", "string003", "string004")

del Tuple

print (Tuple)

OUTPUT – name 'Tuple' is not defined

You can **join multiple Tuples** with the use of the "+" logical operator.

Tuple1 = ("string001", "string002", "string003", "string004")

Tuple2 = (100, 200, 300)

Tuple3 = Tuple1 + Tuple2

print (Tuple3)

OUTPUT – ("string001", "string002", "string003", "string004", 100, 200, 300)

You can also use the "tuple ( )" constructor to create a Tuple, as shown in the example below:

Tuple1 = tuple (("string001", "string002", "string003", "string004"))

print (Tuple1)

EXERCISE – Create a Tuple "X" with string data values as "pies, cake, bread, scone, cookies" and display the item at -3 position.

USE YOUR DISCRETION HERE AND WRITE YOUR CODE FIRST

Now, check your code against the correct code below:

X = ("pies", "cake", "bread", "scone", "cookies")
print (X [-3])

OUTPUT – ("bread")

EXERCISE – Create a Tuple "X" with string data values as "pies, cake, bread, scone, cookies" and display items ranging from -2 to -4.

USE YOUR DISCRETION HERE AND WRITE YOUR CODE FIRST

Now, check your code against the correct code below:
X = ("pies", "cake", "bread", "scone", "cookies")
print (X [-4 : -2])

OUTPUT – ("cake", "bread")

EXERCISE – Create a Tuple "X" with string data values as "pies, cake, bread, scone, cookies" and change its item from "cookies" to "tart" using List function.

USE YOUR DISCRETION HERE AND WRITE YOUR CODE FIRST

Now, check your code against the correct code below:

X = ("pies", "cake", "bread", "scone", "cookies")

Y = list (X)

Y [4] = "tart"

X = tuple (Y)

print (X)

OUTPUT – ("pies", "cake", "bread", "scone", "tart")

EXERCISE – Create a Tuple "X" with string data values as "pies, cake, cookies" and another Tuple "Y" with numeric data values as (2, 12, 22), then join them together.

USE YOUR DISCRETION HERE AND WRITE YOUR CODE FIRST

Now, check your code against the correct code below:

X = ("pies", "cake", "cookies")

Y = (2, 12, 22)

Z = X + Y

print (Z)

OUTPUT – ("pies", "cake", "cookies", 2, 12, 22)

Python Sets

In Python, Sets are collections of data types that cannot be organized and indexed. Sets do not allow for duplicate items and must be written within curly brackets, as shown in the syntax below:

set = {"string1", "string2", "string3"}

print (set)

Unlike the Python List and Tuple, you cannot selectively display desired items from a Set by referencing the position of that item because the Python Set are not arranged in any order. Therefore, items do not have any indexing. However, the "for" loop can be used on Sets (more on this topic later in this chapter).

Unlike Python Lists, you cannot directly **change the data values of Python Sets** after they have been created. However, you can use the "add ()" method to add a single item to Set and use the "update ( )" method to one or more items to an already existing Set. Let's look at the example below:

set = {"string1", "string2", "string3"}

set. add ("newstring")

print (set)

OUTPUT – {"string1", "string2", "string3", "newstring"}

set = {"string1", "string2", "string3"}

set.   update   (["newstring1",   "newstring2",
"newstring3",)

print (set)

OUTPUT   –   {"string1",   "string2",   "string3",
"newstring1", "newstring2", "newstring3"}

You can also determine the **length** of a Python Set
using the "len()" function, as shown in the example
below:

set = {"string1", "string2", "string3", "string4",
"string5", "string6", "string7"}

print (len(set))

OUTPUT – 7

To selectively **delete a specific item from a Set**, the "remove ()" method can be used as shown in the code below:

set = {"string1", "string2", "string3", "string4", "string5"}

set. remove ("string4")

print (set)

OUTPUT – {"string1", "string2", "string3", "string5"}

You can also use the "discard ( )" method to delete specific items from a Set, as shown in the example below:

set = {"string1", "string2", "string3", "string4", "string5"}

set. discard ("string3")

print (set)

OUTPUT – {"string1", "string2", "string4", "string5"}

The "pop ( )" method can be used to selectively delete only the last item of a Set. It must be noted here that since the Python Sets are unordered, any item that the system deems as the last item will be removed. As a result, the output of this method will be the item that has been removed.

```
set = {"string1", "string2", "string3", "string4",
"string5"}
A = set.pop ( )
print (A)
print (set)
```

OUTPUT –
String2
{"string1", "string3", "string4", "string5"}

To delete the entire Set, the "del" keyword can be used, as shown below.

```
set = {"string1", "string2", "string3", "string4",
"string5"}
delete set
print (set)
```

OUTPUT – name 'set' is not defined

To delete all the items from the Set without deleting the variable itself, the "clear ()" method can be used, as shown below:

```
set = {"string1", "string2", "string3", "string4",
"string5"}
```

set.clear ( )

print (set)

OUTPUT – set ( )

You can **join multiple Sets** with the use of the "union ( )" method. The output of this method will be a new set that contains all items from both the sets. You can also use the "update ( )" method to insert all the items from one set into another without creating a new Set.

Set1 = {"string1", "string2", "string3", "string4", "string5"}

Set2 = {15, 25, 35, 45, 55}

Set3 = Set1.union (Set2)

print (Set3)

OUTPUT – {"string1", 15, "string2", 25, "string3", 35, "string4", 45, "string5", 55}

Set1 = {"string1", "string2", "string3", "string4", "string5"}

Set2 = {15, 25, 35, 45, 55}

Set1.update (Set2)

print (Set1)

OUTPUT – *{25, "string1", 15, "string4",55, "string2", 35, "string3", 45, "string5"}*

You can also use the "set ( )" constructor to create a Set, as shown in the example below:

Set1 = set (("string1", "string2", "string3", "string4", "string5"))

print (Set1)

OUTPUT – {"string3", "string5", "string2", "string4", "string1"}

EXERCISE – Create a Set "Veg" with string data values as "pies, cake, bread, scone, cookies" and add new items "tart", "custard" and "waffles" to this Set.

USE YOUR DISCRETION HERE AND WRITE YOUR CODE FIRST

Now, check your code against the correct code below:

Veg = {"pies", "cake", "bread", "scone", "cookies"}

Veg.update (["tart", "custard", "waffles"])

print (Veg)

OUTPUT – {"pies", "custard", "scone", "cake", "bread", "waffles", "cookies", "tart"}

EXERCISE – Create a Set "Veg" with string data values as "pies, cake, bread, scone, cookies", then delete the last item from this Set.

USE YOUR DISCRETION HERE AND WRITE YOUR CODE FIRST

Now, check your code against the correct code below:

Veg = {"pies", "cake", "bread", "scone", "cookies"}

X = Veg.pop ( )

print (X)

print (Veg)

OUTPUT –

bread

{"pies", "scone", "cake", "cookies"}

EXERCISE – Create a Set "Veg" with string data values as "pies, cake, bread, scone, cookies" and another Set

"Veg2" with items as "tart, eggos, custard, waffles". Then combine both these Sets to create a third new Set.

*** USE YOUR DISCRETION HERE AND WRITE YOUR CODE FIRST ***

Now, check your code against the correct code below:

Veg = {"pies", "cake", "bread", "scone", "cookies"}
Veg2 = {"tart", "eggos", "custard", "waffles"}

AllVeg = Veg.union (Veg2)   #this Set name may vary as it has not been defined in the exercise

print (AllVeg)

OUTPUT – {"pies", "custard", "scone", "cake", "eggos", "bread", "waffles", "cookies", "tart"}

Python Dictionary

In Python, Dictionaries are collections of data types that can be changed and indexed but are not arranged in any order. Each item in a Python Dictionary will comprise a key and its value. Dictionaries do not allow for duplicate items and must be written within curly brackets, as shown in the syntax below:

dict = {

"key01": "value01",

"key02": "value02",

"key03": "value03",

}

print (dict)

You can selectively display desired item value from a Dictionary by referencing its key inside square brackets in the print command as shown below:

dict = {

"key01": "value01",

"key02": "value02",

"key03": "value03",

}

X = dict ["key02"]

print (X)

OUTPUT – value02

You can also use the "get ( )" method to view the value of a key, as shown in the example below:

dict = {

"key01": "value01",

"key02": "value02",

"key03": "value03",

}

X = dict.get ("key01")

print (X)

OUTPUT – value01

There might be instances when you need to **change the value** of a key in a Python Dictionary. This can be accomplished by referring to the key of that item and declaring the new value. Let's look at the example below:

dict = {

"key01": "value01",

"key02": "value02",

"key03": "value03",

}

dict ["key03"] = "NEWvalue"

print (dict)

OUTPUT – {"key01": "value01", "key02": "value02", "key03": "NEWvalue"}

You can also determine the **length** of a Python Dictionary using the "len()" function, as shown in the example below:

dict = {

"key01": "value01",

"key02": "value02",

"key03": "value03",

"key04": "value04",

"key05": "value05"

}

print (len (dict))

OUTPUT – 5

Python Dictionary can also be changed by **adding** new index key and assigning a new value to that key, as shown in the example below:

dict = {

"key01": "value01",
"key02": "value02",
"key03": "value03",
}

dict ["NEWkey"] = "NEWvalue"
print (dict)

OUTPUT – {"key01": "value01", "key02": "value02", "key03": "value03", "NEWkey": "NEWvalue"}

There are multiple built-in methods to **delete items** from a Python Dictionary.

- To selectively delete a specific item value, the "pop ()" method can be used with the indicated key name.

dict = {
"key01": "value01",
"key02": "value02",
"key03": "value03",
}
dict.pop ("key01")

print (dict)

OUTPUT – { "key02": "value02", "key03": "value03"}

- To selectively delete the item value that was last inserted, the "popitem ()" method can be used with the indicated key name.

dict = {
"key01": "value01",
"key02": "value02",
"key03": "value03",
}
dict.popitem ( )
print (dict)

OUTPUT – { "key01": "value01", "key02": "value02"}

- To selectively delete a specific item value, the "del" keyword can also be used with the indicated key name.

dict = {
"key01": "value01",

"key02": "value02",

"key03": "value03",

}

del dict ("key03")

print (dict)

OUTPUT – { "key01": "value01", "key02": "value02"}

- To delete a Python Dictionary in its entirety, the "del" keyword can also be used as shown in the example below:

dict = {

"key01": "value01",

"key02": "value02",

"key03": "value03",

}

del dict

print (dict)

OUTPUT – name 'dict' is not defined

- To delete all the items from the Dictionary without deleting the Dictionary itself, the "clear ()" method can be used as shown below:

```
dict = {
"key01": "value01",
"key02": "value02",
"key03": "value03",
}
dict.clear ( )
print (dict)
```

OUTPUT – { }

There might be instances when you need to **copy** an existing Python Dictionary. This can be accomplished by using the built-in "copy ( )" method or the "dict ( )" method, as shown in the examples below:

```
dict = {
"key01": "value01",
"key02": "value02",
"key03": "value03",
}
newdict = dict.copy ( )
print (newdict)
OUTPUT – {"key01": "value01", "key02": "value02",
"key03": "value03"}
```

```
Olddict = {
"key01": "value01",
"key02": "value02",
"key03": "value03",
}
newdict = dict (Olddict )
print (newdict)
```

OUTPUT – {"key01": "value01", "key02": "value02", "key03": "value03"}

There is a unique feature that supports multiple Python Dictionaries to be **nested** within another Python Dictionary. You can either create a Dictionary containing child Dictionaries, as shown in the example below:

```
WendysFamilyDict = {
"burger1" : {
"name" : "Hamburger",
"price" : 2.99
},
"burger2" : {
"name" : "Cheeseburger",
"price" : 5
},
```

```
"burger3" : {
"name" : "Bigburger",
"price" : 1.99
}
}
print (WendysFamilyDict)
```

OUTPUT - {"burger1" : { "name" : "Hamburger", "price" : 2.99}, "burger2" : {"name" : "Cheeseburger", "price" : 5}, "burger3" : {"name" : "Bigburger", "price" : 1.99}}

Or you can create a brand new Dictionary that contain other Dictionaries already existing on the system; your code will look like the one below:

```
burgerDict1 : {
"name" : "Hamburger",
"price" : 2.99
}

burgerDict2 : {
"name" : "Cheeseburger",
"price" : 5
}
```

```
burgerDict3 : {
"name" : "Bigburger",
"price" : 1.99
}

WendysFamilyDict = {
"burgerDict1" : burgerDict1,
"burgerDict2" : burgerDict2
"burgerDict3" : burgerDict3
}
print (WendysFamilyDict)
```

OUTPUT - {"burger1" : { "name" : "Hamburger", "price" : 2.99}, "burger2" : {"name" : "Cheeseburger", "price" : 5}, "burger3" : {"name" : "Bigburger", "price" : 1.99}}

Lastly, you can use the "dict ( )" function to create a new Python Dictionary. The key differences when you create items for the Dictionary using this function are 1. Round brackets are used instead of the curly brackets. 2. Equal to sign is used instead of the semi-colon. Let's look at the example below:

DictwithFunction = dict (key01 = "value01", key02 = "value02", key03 = "value03")

   print (DictwithFunction)

OUTPUT – {"key01": "value01", "key02": "value02", "key03": "value03"}

EXERCISE – Create a Dictionary "Hortons" with items containing keys as "type", "size" and "price" with corresponding values as "cappuccino", "grande" and "4.99". Then add a new item with key as "syrup" and value as "hazelnut".

USE YOUR DISCRETION HERE AND WRITE YOUR CODE FIRST

Now, check your code against the correct code below:

```
Hortons = {
"type" : "cappuccino",
"size" : "grande",
"price" : 4.99
}
Hortons ["syrup"] = "hazelnut"
print (Hortons)
```

OUTPUT – {"type" : "cappuccino", "size" : "grande", "price" : 4.99, "syrup" : "hazelnut"}

EXERCISE – Create a Dictionary "Hortons" with items containing keys as "type", "size", and "price" with corresponding values as "cappuccino", "grande" and "4.99". Then use a function to remove the last added item.

USE YOUR DISCRETION HERE AND WRITE YOUR CODE FIRST

Now, check your code against the correct code below:
```
Hortons = {
"type" : "cappuccino",
"size" : "grande",
"price" : 4.99
}
Hortons.popitem ( )
print (Hortons)
OUTPUT – {"type" : "cappuccino", "size" : "grande"}
```

EXERCISE – Create a Dictionary "Hortons" with nested dictionary as listed below:

Dictionary Name	Key	Value
Coffee01	name	cappuccino
	size	venti
Coffee02	name	frappe
	size	grande
Coffee03	name	macchiato
	size	small

USE YOUR DISCRETION HERE AND WRITE YOUR CODE FIRST

Now, check your code against the correct code below:

```
Hortons = {
"coffee01" : {
"name" : "cappuccino",
"size" : "venti"
},
"coffee02" : {
"name" : "frappe",
"size" : "grande"
},
"coffee03" : {
"name" : "macchiato",
"size" : "small"
```

```
}
}
print (Hortons)
```

OUTPUT - {"coffee01" : { "name" : "cappuccino", "size" : "venti"}, "coffee02" : {"name" : "frappe", "size" : "grande"}, "coffee03" : {"name" : "macchiato", "size" : "small"}}

EXERCISE – Use the "dict ()" function to create a Dictionary "Hortons" with items containing keys as "type", "size" and "price" with corresponding values as "cappuccino", "grande" and "4.99".

USE YOUR DISCRETION HERE AND WRITE YOUR CODE FIRST

Now, check your code against the correct code below:
```
Hortons = dict (type = "cappuccino", size = "grande", price = 4.99}
print (Hortons)
```
OUTPUT – {"type" : "cappuccino", "size" : "grande", "price" : 4.99, "syrup" : "hazelnut"}

Day 4: Advance Python Concepts

Python Conditions and If statement

Python allows the usage of multiple mathematical, logical conditions as listed below:

- Equal to – "a == y"
- Not equal – "a !=y"
- Less than – "a < y"
- Less than, equal to – "a <= y"
- Greater than – "a > y"
- Greater than, equal to – "a >=y"

If Statement

All these conditions can be used within loops and **"if statement"**. The "if" keyword must be used to write these statements, as shown in the syntax below:

X = numeric1

Y = numeric2

if X > Y:

    print ("X is greater than Y")

The most important thing to remember here is that the indentation or the blank space at the beginning of a line in the code above is critical. Unlike other programming languages that use curly brackets, Python programming is driven by indentation in the process of defining the scope of the code. Therefore, writing the Python code below will result in an error.

```
X = numeric1
Y = numeric2
if X > Y:
print ("X is greater than Y")        #leads to an error
```

Else-if Statement

You can use the "elif" keyword to evaluate if the preceding condition is not true, then execute the subsequent condition. Here is the syntax followed by an example to help you understand this concept further:

```
X = numeric1
Y = numeric2
if X > Y:
    print ("X is greater than Y")
elif X == Y:
    print ("X and Y are equal")
```

Example:

```
X = 58
Y = 58
if X > Y:
    print ("X is greater than Y")
elif X == Y:
    print ("X and Y are equal")


OUTPUT - X and Y are equal
```

Else Statement

You can use the "else" keyword to execute any condition if the preceding conditions are not true. Here is the syntax followed by an example to help you understand this concept further:

```
X = numeric1
Y = numeric2
if X > Y:
    print ("X is greater than Y")
elif X == Y:
    print ("X and Y are equal")
else:
    print ("Y is greater than X")
```

Example:

```
X = 58
Y = 59
if X > Y:
    print ("X is greater than Y")
elif X == Y:
    print ("X and Y are equal")
else:
    print ("Y is greater than X")
```

OUTPUT - Y is greater than X

Alternatively, you can use the "else" keyword without using the "elif" keyword, as shown in the example below:

```
X = 69
Y = 96
if X > Y:
    print ("X is greater than Y")
else:
    print ("X is not greater than Y")
```

OUTPUT - X is not greater than Y

Single Line If Statement

You could even execute single line statements with "If" clause, as shown in the syntax below:

If x > y: print ("y is greater than x")

Single Line If-Else Statement

You could even execute single line statements with "If - Else" clause, as shown in the syntax below:

x = 10

y = 15

print ("x") If x > y else print ("y")

Single Line If-Else Statement with multiple Else

You will also be able to execute single line statements with "If - Else" clause containing multiple "Else" statements in the same line, as shown in the syntax below:

x = 100

y = 100

print ("x") If x > y else print ("=") if a == b else print ("y")

"And" Keyword

If you are looking to combine multiple conditional statements, you can do so with the use of the "and" keyword, as shown in the example below:

x = 20

y = 18

z = 35

if x > y and z > x :

   print ("All conditions are True")

"Or" Keyword

If you are looking to combine multiple conditional statements, the other way you can do so is with the use of the "or" keyword, as shown in the example below:

x = 20

y = 18

z = 35

if x > y or x > z :

   print ("At least one of the conditions is True")

"Nested If" Statements

You can have multiple "if" statements within an "if" statement, as shown in the example below:

x = 110

```
if x > 50:
    print ("Greater than 50, ")
if x > 90:
    print ("and greater than 100")
else:
    print ("Not greater than 100")
```

"Pass" statements

In Python, if you ever need to execute "if" statements without any content, you must incorporate a "pass" statement to avoid triggering any error. Here is an example to further your understanding of this concept.

```
x = 20
y = 55
if y > x
    pass
```

EXERCISE – Write the code to check if X = 69 is greater than Y = 79, the output should read "X is greater than Y". If the first condition is not true, then check if X is equal to Y, the output should read "X and Y are equal" otherwise the output should read "Y is greater than X".

Now, check your code against the correct code below:

```
X = 69
Y = 79
if X > Y:
    print ("X is greater than Y")
elif X == Y:
    print ("X and Y are equal")
else:
    print ("Y is greater than X")
```

OUTPUT – "Y is greater than X"

EXERCISE – Write the code to check if x = 69 is greater '50', the output should read "Greater than 50". Then check if x is greater than '60', the output should read "And greater than 60", otherwise the output should read "Not greater than 60".

Now, check your code against the correct code below:

x = 69

if x > 50:

    print ("Greater than 50")

if x > 60:

    print ("And greater than 60")

else:

    print ("Not greater than 60")

OUTPUT –

"Greater than 50"

"And greater than 60"

EXERCISE – Write the code to check if x = 9 is greater than y = 19 as well as if z = 25 is greater than x. The output should read if one or both the conditions are true.

USE YOUR DISCRETION HERE AND WRITE YOUR CODE FIRST

Now, check your code against the correct code below:

x = 9

y = 19

```
z = 25
if x > y and z > x :
    print ("Both the conditions are True")
```

OUTPUT – "Both the conditions are True"

EXERCISE – Write the code to check if x = 45 is less than y = 459 or z = 1459 is less than x. The output should read if one or both the conditions are true.

USE YOUR DISCRETION HERE AND WRITE YOUR CODE FIRST

Now, check your code against the correct code below:
```
x = 45
y = 459
z = 1459
if x < y and z < x :
    print ("At least one of the conditions is True")
```

OUTPUT – "At least one of the conditions is True"

Python "While" Loop

Python allows the usage of one of its standard loop commands i.e. "while" loop for execution of a block of statements, given that the initial condition holds true.

Here is the syntax for "while" loop statements:

```
p = num1
while p < num2:
    print (p)
    p += 1
```

In the syntax above, to prevent the loop from continuing with no end, the variable (p) was limited by setting to an increment. It is a pre-requisite for the "while" loop to index the variable in the statement.

"break" statements

These statements allow exiting from the "while" loop, even if the set condition holds true. In the example below, the variable will exit the loop when it reaches 4:

```
p = 2
while p < 7:
    print (p)
    if p == 4
        break
```

p += 2

OUTPUT –

2

3

4

"continue" statements

These statements allow the system to stop the execution of the current condition and move to the next iteration of the loop. In the example below, system will continue the execution of the subsequent command if the variable equals 2:

```
p = 1
while p < 5:
    p += 1
    if p == 2:
        continue
    print (p)
```

OUTPUT –

1

3

4

5

(Note - The number 2 is missing from the result above)

"else" statement

The "else" statement allows you to execute a set of code after the "while" condition doesn't hold true any longer. The output in the example below will include a statement that the initial condition is no longer true:

```
p = 1
while p < 5:
    print (p)
    p += 1
else:
    print ("p is no longer less than 5")
```

OUTPUT –

1

2

3

4

p is no longer less than 5

EXERCISE – Write the code to print a series of number if x = 1 is smaller than 7.

USE YOUR DISCRETION HERE AND WRITE YOUR CODE FIRST

Now, check your code against the correct code below:

```
x = 1
while x < 7:
    print (x)
    x += 1
```

OUTPUT –

1

2

3

4

5

6

EXERCISE – Write the code to print a series of number if x = 1 is smaller than 6 and exit the loop when x is 3.

*** *USE YOUR DISCRETION HERE AND WRITE YOUR CODE FIRST* ***

Now, check your code against the correct code below:

```
x = 1
while x < 6:
    print (x)
    if x == 3
        break
    x += 1
```

OUTPUT –

1

2

3

EXERCISE – Write the code to print a series of number if x = 1 is smaller than 6 and continue to execute the initial condition if x is 3 in a new iteration.

*** *USE YOUR DISCRETION HERE AND WRITE YOUR CODE FIRST* ***

Now, check your code against the correct code below:

```
x = 1
while x < 6:
    x += 1
    if x == 3:
    continue
    print (x)
```

OUTPUT –

1

2

4

5

6

(Note – The number 3 is missing, but the initial condition is executed in a new iteration.)

EXERCISE – Write the code to print a series of number if x = 1 is smaller than 4. Once this condition turns false, print "x is no longer less than 4".

USE YOUR DISCRETION HERE AND WRITE YOUR CODE FIRST

Now, check your code against the correct code below:

```
x = 1
while x < 4:
    print (x)
    x = 1
else:
    print ("x is no longer less than 4")
```

OUTPUT –

1

2

3

x is no longer less than 4

Python "For" Loop

Another one of the Python standard loops is "for" loop, which is used to execute iterations over a series such as string, tuple, set, dictionary, list. The "for" keyword in Python functions like an iterator found in object-oriented programming languages. It allows the execution of a block of statements once for every single item of tuple, set, list, and other series.

Let's look at the example below:

```
veg = ["tart", "scone", "cookies"]
for X in veg:
    print (X)
```

OUTPUT –

tart

scone

cookies

You will notice that in the code above that the variable was not defined. The "for" loop can be executed without setting an index for the variable in the code.

Loops for String

Python strings constitute a series of characters are iterative in nature. So if you wanted to loop through characters of a string, you could simply use the "for" loop as shown in the example below:

```
for X in "carrot":
    print (X)
```

OUTPUT –

c

a

r

r

o

t

"break" statements

If you want to exit the loop prior to its completion, you can use the "break" statements as shown in the example below:

veg = ["tart", "scone", "cookies", "pies", "carrot"]

for X in veg:

    print (X)

    if X == "pies":

    break

OUTPUT –

tart

scone

cookies

pies

In the example below, the print command was executed prior to the "break" statement and directly affected the output:

```
veg = ["tart", "scone", "cookies", "pies", "carrot"]
for X in veg:
    if X == "pies":
          break
print (X)
```

OUTPUT –
tart
scone
cookies

"continue" statement

Similar to the "while" loop, the "continue" statements in the "for" loop is used to stop the execution of the current condition and move to the next iteration of the loop. Let's looks at the example below to further understand this concept:

```
veg = ["tart", "scone", "cookies", "pies", "carrot"]
for X in veg:
    if X == "cookies":
          continue
print (X)
```

OUTPUT –

tart

scone

pies

carrot

"range" function

The "range ( )" function can be used to loop through a block of code for a specific number of times. This function will result in a series of number beginning with "0" by default, with regular increments of 1 and ending at a specific number.

Here is an example of this function:

for X in range (5):

    print (X)

OUTPUT –

0

1

2

3

4

Note – The "range ( )" function defaulted to 0 as the first output, and the final value of the range, 5, is excluded from the output.

Let's look at another example with a start and end value of the "range ( )" function:

for X in range (1, 5):

print (X)

OUTPUT –

1

2

3

4

In the example below, we will specify the increment value, which is set to 1 by default:

for X in range (3, 20, 5):

print (X)

OUTPUT –

3

8

13

18

"Else" in "For" Loop

You can use the "else" keyword to specify a set of code that need to be executed upon the completion of the loop, as shown in the example below:

for X in range (5):

   print (X)

else:

   print ("The loop was completed")

OUTPUT –

0

1

2

3

4

The loop was completed

"Nested" Loops

When loops are defined within a loop, execution of the inner loop will occur once for each iteration of the outer loop. Let's look at the example below, where we want every single adjective must be printed for each listed vegetable:

adjective = ["olive", "leafy", "healthy"]

veg = ["spinach", "kale", "asparagus"]

for X in adjective:

    for Y in veg:

        print (X, Y)

OUTPUT –

olive spinach

olive kale

olive asparagus

leafy spinach

leafy kale

leafy asparagus

healthy spinach

healthy kale

healthy asparagus

"pass" statements

In Python, if you ever need to execute "for" loops without any content, you must incorporate a "pass" statement to avoid triggering any error. Here is an example to further your understanding of this concept.

```
for X in [ 1, 2, 3]
    pass
```

OUTPUT - ......

The empty "for" loop code above would have resulted in an error without the "pass" statement.

EXERCISE – Write the code to loop through a list of colors ("cyan", "lilac", "red") without defining a variable. Then loop through the characters of the string "cyan".

USE YOUR DISCRETION HERE AND WRITE YOUR CODE FIRST

Now, check your code against the correct code below:

```
colors = ["cyan", "lilac", "red"]
for A in colors:
    print (A)
for B in "cyan":
    print (B)
```

OUTPUT –

cyan

lilac

red

c

y

a

n

EXERCISE – Write the code to loop through a list of colors ("cyan", "lilac", "red", "white") without defining a variable. Then break the loop at "red", without printing it in the result.

USE YOUR DISCRETION HERE AND WRITE YOUR CODE FIRST

Now, check your code against the correct code below:

colors = ["cyan", "lilac", "red", "white"]

for A in colors:

    if A == "red":

        break

    print (A)

OUTPUT –

cyan

lilac

EXERCISE – Write the code to loop through a range of numbers starting with 5 and ending with 30. Make sure to define the increments at 6.

USE YOUR DISCRETION HERE AND WRITE YOUR CODE FIRST

Now, check your code against the correct code below:

for X in range (5, 30, 6):

   print (X)

OUTPUT –

5

11

16

22

28

EXERCISE – Write the code to loop phones ("iPhone", "Samsung", "Google"), and loop that with colors ("black", "white", "gold") using nested loops.

USE YOUR DISCRETION HERE AND WRITE YOUR CODE FIRST

Now, check your code against the correct code below:
colors = ["black", "white", "gold"]
phones = ["iPhone", "Samsung", "Google"]

for X in colors:
    for Y in phones:
    print (X, Y)

OUTPUT –
black iPhone
black Samsung
black Google
white iPhone
white Samsung
white Google
gold iPhone
gold Samsung

Python Classes and Objects

Python is one of the many object oriented coding languages. Every entity of Python can be considered an object and has its own methods and properties. In Python, Classes are used to construct these objects serving as object blueprints.

A Python Class can be created using the keyword "class" with a predefined property (p) as shown in the syntax below:

class ClassName:

    p = 2

A Python Object can then be created from the Python Class created above, as shown in the syntax below:

Object1 = ClassName ( )

print (object1.p)

Built-in Function

In reality, creation of classes and objects is much more complex than the basic syntax provided above. This is where a built-in function to create classes called "__init__()" is used. When the classes are being created, this inherent class function is executed with it. The "__init__()" function is mostly used for assigning values to object properties and other actions that are required for creation of an object. Let's look at the example below to understand this function:

class Vehicle:

    def __init__ (self, name, year)

    self.name = name

    self.name = year

  v1 = Vehicle ("AUDI", 2018)

  print (v1.name)

  print (v1.year)

OUTPUT – AUDI   2018

Object Methods

There are certain methods that can be created with the Python Objects. These methods can be considered as functions of that object. For example, to create a function that would print a comment regarding ownership of the vehicle and executed on the object v1, the command below will be used:

class Vehicle:

    def __init__ (self, name, year)

    self.name = name

    self.name = year

def newfunc (ownership):

    print ("I am a proud owner of " + self.name)

v1 = Vehicle ("AUDI", 2018)

v1.newfunc ()

OUTPUT – I am a proud owner of AUDI

Reference Parameter

To refer to the latest instance of a class, the "self" parameter is used. It allows you to access variables that have been derived from a class. This parameter can be named as needed and does not have to be named "self". The important thing to remember here is that the first parameter defined for a class will become the reference parameter for that class, as shown in the example below:

    class Vehicle:

```
        def __init__ (refobject, name, year)
        refobject.name = name
        refobject.name = year


def newfunc (xyz):
        print ("I am a proud owner of " + xyz.name)


v1 = Vehicle ("AUDI", 2018)
v1.newfunc ()


OUTPUT – I am a proud owner of AUDI
```

There might be instances when you need to **change the properties** of an object. You can easily do so by declaring the new property of the object as shown in the example below:

```
class Vehicle:
        def __init__ (refobject, name, year)
        refobject.name = name
        refobject.name = year


def newfunc (xyz):
        print ("I am a proud owner of " + xyz.name)
```

v1 = Vehicle ("AUDI", 2018)

v1.year = 2019

You can use the "del" keyword to selectively **remove properties of an object**, as shown in the example below:

class Vehicle:

    def __init__ (refobject, name, year)

    refobject.name = name

    refobject.name = year

def newfunc (xyz):

    print ("I am a proud owner of " + xyz.name)

v1 = Vehicle ("AUDI", 2018)

del v1.year

print (v1.age)

OUTPUT – 'Vehicle' object has no 'year' attribute

You can also use the "del" keyword to entirely **delete an object**, as shown in the example below:

```
class Vehicle:
    def __init__ (refobject, name, year)
    refobject.name = name
    refobject.name = year


def newfunc (xyz):
    print ("I am a proud owner of " + xyz.name)


v1 = Vehicle ("AUDI", 2018)


del v1


OUTPUT – NameError: 'v1' is not defined
```

The "pass" statement

The definition of a Python Class must contain values, or you will receive an error. However, there might be instances when the definition of a class does not have any content. In such a case, you can use the "pass" statement to avoid getting an error. Look at the example below:

```
class Vehicle:   # this class definition is empty
    pass         # used to avoid any errors
```

EXERCISE – Create a Class "KafeShop" with properties as "type" and "size" with corresponding values as "cappuccino" and "large", respectively.

USE YOUR DISCRETION HERE AND WRITE YOUR CODE FIRST

Now, check your code against the correct code below:
class KafeShop:

    def __init__ (refobject, type, size)

    refobject.type = type

    refobject.size = size

c1 = KafeShop ("cappuccino", "large")

print (c1.type)

print (c1.size)

OUTPUT – cappuccino   *large*

EXERCISE – Create a Class "KafeShop" with properties as "type" and "size" with corresponding values as "cappuccino" and "large" respectively. Create a new function "funct1" that would print "I would like to order a" and execute it on the object.

Now, check your code against the correct code below:

class KafeShop:

    def __init__ (refobject, type, size)

    refobject.type = type

    refobject.size = size

    def funct1 (refobject):

    print ("I would like to order a" + refobject.type)

c1 = KafeShop ("cappuccino", "large")

c1.funct1 ( )

OUTPUT – I would like to order a cappuccino

Python Operators

In Python, a variety of Operators can be used to perform operations on a Python variable and its values. The different groups of Python operators are provided below:

Arithmetic Operators can be utilized with numerical values to execute basic math calculations.

Name	Operator	Sample
Add	+	J + K
Subtract	-	J - K
Multiply	*	J * K
Divide	/	J / K
Modulus	%	J % K
Exponentiation	**	J ** K
Floor division	//	J // K

Assignment Operators can be utilized for the assignment of values to a variable.

Name	Sample
=	J = 5
+=	J += 3
-=	J -= 3
*=	J *= 3
/=	J /= 3
%=	J %= 3
//=	J //= 3
**=	J **= 3
&=	J &= 3

|=	J |= 3
^=	J ^= 3
>>=	J >>= 3
<<=	J <<= 3

Comparison Operators can be utilized to draw a comparison between the values.

Name	Operator	Sample
Equal	==	J == K
Not equal	!=	J != K
Greater than	>	J > K
Less than	<	J < K
Greater than or equal to	>=	J >= K
Less than or equal to	<=	J <= K

Logical Operators can be utilized to generate a combination of conditional statements.

Operator	Usage	Sample
and	Will return "True" if both the statements hold true.	J < 5 and J < 10
or	Will return "True" if one of the statements holds true.	J < 5 or J < 4

| not | Will reverse the results and return "False" if the results are true. | Not (J < 5 and J < 10) |

Identity Operators can be utilized to draw a comparison between two objects to check whether the same object was created more than once using the same memory location.

Operator	Usage	Sample
is	Will return true if the two variables are the same object.	J is K
is not	Will return true if the two variables are not the same object.	J is not K

Membership Operators can be utilized to test if select sequence can be found in an object.

Operator	Usage	Sample
in	Will return True if a sequence with a specific value can be found in the object.	J in K

not in	Will return True if a sequence with a specific value cannot be found in the object.	J not in K

Bitwise Operators can be utilized to draw a comparison between two numeric values.

Operator	Usage	Sample
&	AND	Will set each bit to 1 if the two bits are 1
|	OR	Will set each bit to 1 if one of the two bits is 1
^	XOR	Will set each bit to 1 if only one of the two bits is 1
~	NOT	Will invert all the bits
<<	Zero fill left shift	Shifts left by pushing zero in from the right, making the left most bit to be dropped
>>	Signed right shift	Shifts right by pushing copies of the left most bit in from the left, making the right most bit to be dropped

Day 5: Built-In Functions

Like most programming languages, Python boasts a number of built-in functions to make your life easier while coding a software program. Here is a list of all such built-in functions:

Function	Description
abs ()	Will result in the absolute values of the numbers.
all ()	Will result in True if all items within an iterative object are true.
any ()	Will result in True if any item of the iterative object holds true.
ascii ()	Will result in a readable version of an object and replace non-ascii characters with escape characters.
bin ()	Will result in the binary version of the numbers.
bool ()	Will result in the boolean values of indicated objects.
bytearray ()	Will result in an array of bytes.
bytes ()	Will result in bytes objects.
callable ()	Will result in True if a specific object is callable or else results in False.

chr ()	Will result in a character from the indicated Unicode code.
classmethod ()	Will convert any method into class method.
compile ()	Will result in the indicated source as an object, ready for execution.
complex ()	Will result in a complex number.
delattr ()	Will delete specific attributes (property or method) from the indicated object.
dict ()	Will result in a dictionary.
dir ()	Will result in a list of properties and methods of the specific object.
divmod ()	Will result in the quotient and the remainder when one argument is divided by another.
enumerate ()	Will take a collection and result in enumerate objects.
eval ()	Will evaluate and execute an expression.
exec ()	Will execute the indicated code (or object)
filter ()	Uses a filter function to exclude items in an iterative object.
float ()	Will result in floating point numbers.
format ()	Will format the indicated value.
frozenset ()	Will result in a frozen set object.

getattr ()	Will result in the value of the indicated attribute (property or method).
globals ()	Will result in the most recent global symbol table as a dictionary.
hasattr ()	Will result in True if the indicated object has the indicated attribute.
hash ()	Will result in the hash value of the indicated object.
help ()	Will execute the built-in help system.
hex ()	Conversion of numbers into hexadecimal values.
id ()	Will result in the identity of an object.
input ()	Will allow user input.
int ()	Will result in an integer number.
isinstance ()	Will result in True if the indicated object is an instance of the indicated object.
issubclass ()	Will result in True if the indicated class is a subclass of the indicated object.
iter ()	Will result in an iterative object.
len ()	Will result in the length of an object.
list ()	Will result in a list.
locals ()	Will result in an updated dictionary of the current local symbol table.
map ()	Will result in the indicated iterator with the indicated function applied to each item.

max ()	Will result in the largest item of an iteration.
memoryview ()	Will result in memory view objects.
min ()	Will result in the smallest item of an iteration.
next ()	Will result in the next item in an iteration.
object ()	Will result in a new object.
oct ()	Converts a number into an octet.
open ()	Will open files and result in file objects.
ord ()	Conversion of an integer representing the Unicode of the indicated character.
pow ()	Will result in the value of a to the power of b.
print ()	Will print to the standard output device.
property ()	Will retrieve, set, and delete a property.
range ()	Will result in a sequence of numbers, beginning from 0 and increments of 1.
repr ()	Will result in a readable version of objects.
reversed ()	Will result in a reversed iteration.
round ()	Rounding of a number.
set ()	Will result in new set objects.
setattr ()	Will set attributes of the objects.
slice ()	Will result in a sliced objects.

sorted ()	Will result in sorted lists.
staticmethod ()	Will convert methods into a static method.
str ()	Will result in string objects.
sum ()	Will sum the items of iterations.
super ()	Will result in an object representing the parent class.
tuple ()	Will result in tuples.
type ()	Will result in the type of objects.
vars ()	Will result in the _dict_ property of objects.
zip ()	Will result in a single iteration from multiple iterations.

Python Built-in String methods

There are a number of built-in Python methods specifically for strings of data, which will result in new values for the string without making any changes to the original string. Here is a list of all such methods.

Method	Description
capitalize ()	Will convert the initial character to upper case.
casefold ()	Will convert strings into lower case.

center ()	Will result in centered strings.
count ()	Will result in the number of times an indicated value appears in a string.
encode ()	Will result in an encoded version of the strings.
endswith ()	Will result in true if the string ends with the indicated value.
expandtabs ()	Will set the tab size of the string.
find ()	Will search the string for indicated value and result in its position.
format ()	Will format indicated values of strings.
format_map ()	Will format indicated values of strings.
index ()	Will search the string for indicated value and result in its position.
isalnum ()	Will result in True if all string characters are alphanumeric.
isalpha ()	Will result in True if all string characters are alphabets.
isdecimal ()	Will result in True if all string characters are decimals.
isdigit ()	Will result in True if all string characters are digits.
isidentifier ()	Will result in True if the strings is an identifier.

islower ()	Will result in True if all string characters are lower case.
isnumeric ()	Will result in True if all string characters are numeric.
isprintable ()	Will result in True if all string characters are printable.
isspace ()	Will result in True if all string characters are whitespaces.
istitle ()	Will result in True if the string follows the rules of a title.
isupper ()	Will result in True if all string characters are upper case.
join ()	Will join the elements of an iteration to the end of the string.
ljust ()	Will result in a left-justified version of the string.
lower ()	Will convert a string into lower case.
lstrip ()	Will result in a left trim version of the string.
maketrans ()	Will result in a translation table to be used in translations.
partition ()	Will result in a tuple where the string is separated into 3 sections.
replace ()	Will result in a string where an indicated value is replaced with another indicated value.

rfind ()	Will search the string for an indicated value and result in its last position.
rindex ()	Will search the string for an indicated value and result in its last position.
rjust ()	Will result in the right justified version of the string.
rpartition ()	Will result in a tuple where the string is separated into 3 sections.
rsplit ()	Will split the string at the indicated separator and result in a list.
rstrip ()	Will result in a new string version that has been trimmed at its right.
split ()	Will split the string at the indicated separator and result in a list.
splitlines ()	Will split the string at line breaks and result in a list.
startswith ()	Will result in true if the string starts with the indicated value.
strip ()	Will result in a trimmed version of the string.
swapcase ()	Will swap the alphabet cases.
title ()	Will convert the first character of each word to upper case.
translate ()	Will result in a translated string.
upper ()	Will convert a string into upper case.
zfill ()	Will fill the string with the indicated

	number of 0 values at the beginning.

Python Random Numbers

A "random ()" function does not exist in Python, but it has an embedded module called "random" that may be utilized to create numbers randomly when needed. For instance, if you wanted to call the "random" module and display a number randomly between 100 and 500, you can accomplish this by executing the code below:

import random

print (random.randrange (100, 500))

OUTPUT – Any number between 100 and 500 will be randomly displayed.

There are a number of defined methods in the random module as listed below:

Method	Description
betavariate ()	Will result in random float numbers between 0 and 1 based on the Beta distribution.
choice ()	Will result in random elements on the basis of the provided sequence.

choices ()	Will result in a list consisting of a random selection from the provided sequence.
expovariate ()	Will result in a float number randomly displayed between 0 and -1, or between 0 and 1 for negative parameters on the basis of the statistical exponential distributions.
gammavariate ()	Will result in a float number displayed between 0 and 1 on the basis of the statistical Gamma distribution.
gauss ()	Will result in a float number displayed between 0 and 1 on the basis of the Gaussian distribution, which is widely utilized in probability theory.
getrandbits ()	Will result in a number that represents the random bits.
getstate ()	Will result in the current internal state of the random number generator.
lognormvariate ()	Will result in a float number randomly displayed between 0 and 1 on the basis of a log-normal distribution, which is widely utilized in probability theory.
normalvariate()	Will result in a float number randomly displayed between 0 and 1 on the basis of the normal distribution, which is

	widely utilized in probability theory.
paretovariate()	Will result in a float number randomly displayed between 0 and 1 on the basis of the Pareto distribution, which is widely utilized in probability theory.
randint ()	Will result in a random number between the provided range.
random ()	Will result in a float number randomly displayed between 0 and 1.
randrange ()	Will result in a random number between the provided range.
sample ()	Will result in a sample of the sequences.
seed ()	Will trigger the random number generator.
setstate ()	Will restore the internal state of the random number generator.
shuffle ()	Will take a sequence and result in a sequence but in some random order.
triangular ()	Will result in a random float number between two provided parameters. You could also set a mode parameter for specification of the midpoint between the two other parameters.
uniform ()	Will result in a random float number between two provided parameters.

vonmisesvariate()	Will result in a float number randomly displayed between 0 and 1 on the basis of the von "Mises distribution", which is utilized in directional statistics.
weibullvariate()	Will result in a float number randomly displayed between 0 and 1 on the basis of the Weibull distribution, which is utilized in statistics.

Python Built-in List methods

Python supports a number of built-in methods that can be used on lists or arrays, as listed in the table below:

Method	Description
append ()	Will insert an element at the end of the list.
clear ()	Will remove all the list elements.
copy ()	Will result in a replica of the list.
count ()	Will result in the number of elements with the indicated value.
extend ()	Will add the elements of a list (or any iterator), to the end of the current list.
index ()	Will result in the index of the first element with the indicated value.
insert ()	Will add an element at the indicated

	position.
pop ()	Will remove the element at the indicated position.
remove ()	Will remove the first item with the indicated value.
reverse ()	Will reverse the order of the list.
sort ()	Will sort the list.

Python Built-in Tuple methods

Python supports a couple of built-in methods that can be used on tuples, as listed in the table below:

Method	Description
count ()	Will result in the number of times an indicated value appears in the tuple.
index ()	Will search a tuple for the indicated value and result in the position of where the value is found.

Python Built-in Set methods

Python also supports a variety of embedded methods that can be used on sets that are listed in the table below:

Method	Description
"add ()"	Will add an element to the set.
"clear ()"	Will remove all the elements from the set.
"copy ()"	Will result in a replica of the set.
"difference ()"	Will result in a set that contains the difference between 2 or more sets.
"difference_up date ()"	Will remove the items from a set that can be found in another, indicated set.
"discard ()"	Will remove the indicated item.
"intersection ()"	Will result in a set that is the intersection of couple other sets.
"intersection_u pdate ()"	Will remove the items from a set that are not present in another indicated set.
"isdisjoint ()"	Will determine if intersection exists between two sets.
"issubset ()"	Will determine if the identified set contains another set.
"issuperset ()"	Will determine if a different set contain the identified set or not.
"pop ()"	Will remove an element from the set.
"remove ()"	Will remove the indicated element.
"symmetric_dif ference ()"	Will result in a set with the symmetric differences of the two indicated sets.
"symmetric_dif ference_update	Will insert the symmetric differences from the indicated set and other sets.

()"	
"union ()"	Will result in a set containing the union of sets.
"update ()"	Will update the set with the union of the inidcated set and other sets.

Python Built-in Dictionary methods

Python also supports a large number of built-in methods that can be used on dictionaries that are listed in the table below:

Method	Description
clear ()	Will remove all the elements from the dictionary.
copy ()	Will result in a copy of the dictionary.
fromkeys ()	Will result in a dictionary with the indicated keys and values.
get ()	Will result in the values of the indicated key.
items ()	Will result in a list containing a tuple for every key-value pair.
keys ()	Will result in a list containing the keys of the dictionary.
pop ()	Will remove the elements with the indicated key.

popitem ()	Will remove the key value pair that was most recently added.
setdefault ()	Will result in the values of the indicated key. In case the key is not found, a new key will be added with the indicated values.
update ()	Will update the dictionary with the indicated key value pairs.
values ()	Will result in a list of all the values in the dictionary.

Python Built-in File methods

Python also supports a large number of built-in methods that can be used on file objects that are listed in the table below:

Method	Description
close ()	Will close the file
detach ()	Will result in a separate raw stream.
fileno ()	Will result in a number representing the stream, per the operating system processing.
flush ()	Will flush the internal buffer.
isatty ()	Will result in determination if the file stream is interactive.

read ()	Will result in the content of the file.
readable ()	Will result in determination if the file stream is readable or not.
readline ()	Will result in one line from the file.
readlines ()	Will result in a list of lines from the file.
seek ()	Will modify the position of the file.
seekable ()	Will result in determination if the file permits modification of its position.
tell ()	Will result in the current position of the file.
truncate ()	Will change the size of the file to the indicated value.
writeable ()	Will result in determination if the file permits writing over.
write ()	Will write the indicated string to the file.
writelines ()	Will writes a list of strings to the file.

Python Keywords

Python contains some keywords that cannot be used to define a variable or used as a function name or any other unique identifier. These select Python keywords are listed in the table below:

Method	Description
"and"	Logical operator.
"as"	For creating an alias.
"assert"	To debug.
"break"	For breaking out of a loop.
"class"	For defining a class.
"continue"	For continuing to the next iteration of a loop.
"def"	For defining a function.
"del"	For deleting an object.
"elif"	For use in conditional statements, similar to "else if".
"else"	For use in conditional statements.
"except"	For use with exceptions, so the program knows the steps to follow in case of an exception.
"FALSE"	One of the data values assigned only to Boolean data type.
"finally"	For use with exceptions, this set of code would be executed regardless of any occurrences of an exception.
"for"	Used in creation of a "for loop".
"from"	For importing particular part of a module.
"global"	For declaring a global variable.
"if"	For making conditional statements.

"import"	For importing desired module.
"in"	For checking a specific data value within a tuple or a list.
"is"	For testing two variables that may be equal.
"lambda"	For creating an anonymous function.
"None"	For representation of null data value.
"nonlocal"	For declaration of a non-local variable.
"not"	Logical operator.
"or"	Logical operator.
"pass"	Will result in a null statement that would not be executed.
"raise"	Used to raise an exception to the statement.
"result in"	Used for exiting a function and resulting in a data value.
"TRUE"	One of the data values assigned only to Boolean data type.
"try"	Used for making "try except" statements.
"while"	For creating a "while loop".
"with"	Used for simplification of the handling procedure for exceptions.
"yield"	For terminating a function and resulting in a generator.

Review Quiz

Answer the questions below to verify your understanding of the concepts explained in this chapter. The answer key can be found at the end of the quiz.

1. Name the built in function that will allow you to output Boolean values of indicated objects.

2. Name the built in function that will allow you to output a list of properties and methods of the specific object.

3. Name the built in function that will allow you to output an updated dictionary of the current local symbol table.

4. Name the built in function that will allow you to defined the attributes of the objects.

5. Name the built in string method that will allow you to convert the initial character to upper case.

6. Name the built in string method that will allow you to search the string for indicated value and result in its position.

7. Name the built in string method that will allow you to join the elements of an iteration to the end of the string.

8. Name the built in string method that will allow you to replace an indicated value of a string into another one.

9. Name the built in random number method that will allow you to output a list consisting of a random selection from the provided sequence.

10. Name the built in random number method that will allow you to output the current internal state of the random number generator.

11. Name the built in random number method that will allow you to output a float number randomly displayed between 0 and 1.

12. Name the built in random number method that will allow you to output a random float number between two provided parameters.

13. Name the built in list method that will allow you to insert an element at the end of the list.

14. Name the built in list method that will allow you to add the elements of a list (or any iterator), to the end of the current list.

15. Name the built in tuple method that will allow you to output the number of times an indicated value appears in the tuple.

16. Name the built in tuple method that will allow you to search a tuple for the indicated value and result in the position of where the value is found.

17. Name the built in Set method that will allow you to remove all the elements from the set.

18. Name the built in Set method that will allow you to output a set that is the intersection of couple other sets.

19. Name the built in Dictionary method that will allow you to output a dictionary with the indicated keys and values.

20. Name the built in Dictionary method that will allow you to remove the key value pair that was most recently added.

Answer Key

1. bool ( )
2. dir ( )
3. locals ( )
4. setattr ( )
5. capitalize ( )
6. find ( )
7. join ( )
8. replace ( )

9. choices ( )

10. getstate ( )

11. random ( )

12. uniform ( )

13. append ( )

14. extend ( )

15. count ( )

16. index ( )

17. clear ( )

18. intersection ( )

19. fromkeys ( )

20. popitem ( )

Day 6: Web Development

Django

According to the Django Software Foundation, "Django is a free and open-source, high-level Python Web framework that encourages rapid development and clean, pragmatic design. Built by experienced developers, it takes care of much of the hassle of Web development, so you can focus on writing your app without needing to reinvent the wheel". The main objective of Django is to facilitate the development of sophisticated websites that are driven by databases. Its name is credited to the famous guitarist "Django Reinhardt" and was developed in late 2003 by computer scientists at the Lawrence Journal World newspaper, Adrian Holovaty, and Simon Willison. In July 2005, this framework was launched under a BSD license and was rolled up to the management of the "Django Software Foundation" in June 2008.

This framework promotes reusability and easy plugging in the component, fewer codes, limited connection, faster development, and the no repetition principle. "Django" extensively uses Python for the development of configuration documents and data models. It can be equipped with an optional administrative interface, which is dynamically developed by introspection and administrative model configurations, to allow creating, reading, updating and deleting files as needed. Several of the widely renowned websites are based on this framework, such as Public Broadcasting Service, Instagram, Mozilla, Washington Times, Disqus, Bitbucket, and Nextdoor.

Although the fundamental framework of Django has its own naming conventions, like naming the objects that can be called and used to generate views of the HTTP responses, it could still be considered a model-template-view (MTV) architectural pattern. It comprises of an object-relational mapper (ORM) that acts as a mediator between data models (Python classes) and a relational database (Model), a system to process HTTP requests using a web template system or View, and a standard expression driven "URL dispatcher" or "Controller".

The underlying framework also contains the features listed below:

- A standalone and light weight webserver to develop and test the websites.

- A system to serialize and validate HTML forms, which is capable of translating between appropriate database storage values and these forms.

- A template system using the principle of inheritance as found in object oriented programming.

- A caching framework, which is capable of using a variety of caching techniques.

- Support for middleware classes, which are capable of intervening and performing custom tasks at different phases of request processing.

- An integrated dispatch system allowing application components to relay occurrences to one another, through pre-defined signals.

- An internationalization system, which includes translations of various components of Django into a multitude of languages.

- A serialization system, which is capable of producing and reading XML and/or JSON representations of the Django model instances

- A system that allows extension of the template engine functionality.

- An interface to the integrated unit test framework of Python.

- "Django REST Framework" constitutes a strong and adaptable "Web API construction" toolkit.

Installing Django

All web applications and/or websites developed using Django contains 3 different layers, namely, model, view and controller pertaining to the database, its appearance and logic respectively. This is also referred to as the "MVC" or model view controller architecture. Now, let's start with the installation of Django on your system by running the Python file below:

"pip install Django == 1.7.2"

Now let's generate the directory "/Django-welcome/" for the application and create a new file called welcome.py using the code below:

```python
#!/usr/bin/env python
import sys
from django.conf import settings
from django.conf.urls import patterns
from django.http import HttpResponse
from django.core.management import
execute_from_command_line

settings.configure(
DEBUG = True,
SECRET_KEY = 'asecretkey',
ROOT_URLCONF = sys.modules [__name__],
)

def index(request):
return HttpResponse ('Welcome')

urlpatterns = patterns (' ',
(r'^welcome/$', index),
)

if __name__ == "__main__":
execute_from_command_line (sys.argv)
```

Remember the script you just created can be executed with the command below:

"python welcome.py runserver"

Web application development using Django

In this section we will be creating a web based application to take notes. The first step is creation of the directory "mywebsite" using the Python command below:

"Django-admin startproject mywebsite"

Now, to configure the database as needed, open "mywebsite/mywebsite/settings.py" and execute the code below:

"DATABASES = {
'default': {
'ENGINE': 'django.db.backends.sqlite3',
'NAME': os.path.join(BASE_DIR, 'db.sqlite3'),
}
}"

You can choose from oracle, mysql, or sqlite3 and give desired name to the database. With SQLite the database is created by default. Browse up a directory to /mywebsite/ and execute the command below:

"*python manage.py runserver*"

The terminal will display the code below:

"*Performing system checks...*

System check identified no issues (0 silenced).

You have unapplied migrations; your app may not work properly until they are applied.
Run 'python manage.py migrate' to apply them.

August 16, 2019 - 14:45:29
Django version 1.7.2, using settings 'myapp.settings'
Starting development server at http://127.0.0.1:9000/
Quit the server with CONTROL-C.
[16/Aug/2019 14:45:35] "GET / HTTP/1.1" 200 1759"

If you opened the http in the code above in your web browser, you will see a window similar to the picture shown below:

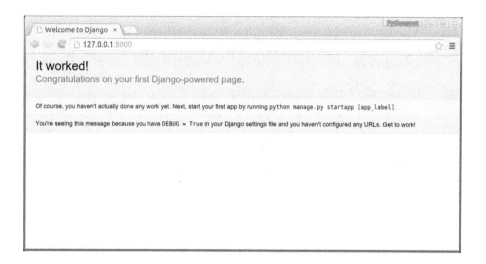

At this point we already have our first project created that is capable of holding multiple applications. So let's create a note taking application by first executing the command below:

"python manage.py startapp notes"

The code above will result in creation of the file below:

"notes/

init.py

admin.py

migrations/

init.py

models.py

tests.py

views.py"

Step 2 is to update the database model to the command below:

"from django.db import models

class Note (models.Model):

text = models.CharField (max_length=120)

created = models.DateTimeField (auto_now_add=True)"

Step 3 is to open the website settings and add the web application using the command below:

"INSTALLED_APPS = (

'django.contrib.admin',

'django.contrib.auth',

'django.contrib.contenttypes',

'django.contrib.sessions',

'django.contrib.messages',

'django.contrib.staticfiles',

'notes'

)"

Step 4 is to update the database by executing "*python manage.py syncdb*" file and then updating the "/mywebsite/mywebsite/admin.py" using the command below:

"from django.contrib import admin

 # Register your models here.
from .models import Note

class NoteAdmin (admin.ModelAdmin):
class Meta:
model = Note

admin.site.register (Note,NoteAdmin)"

Now, you can run the commands below and kickstart the server:

"python manage.py makemigrations notes
python manage.py migrate

manage.py runserver"

As soon as the administration panel is opened up using the defined website address http://127.0.0.1:9000/admin, our browser will appear similar to the picture shown below containing notes administration option:

You can create new notes by clicking on the "Notes" button the page above. You will also be able to view all the notes that have been created and edit them accordingly. The picture below provides a sample of content viewing page of the Notes folder.

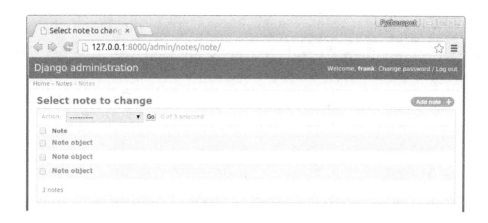

At this stage we have already added required data to the database and can **develop** the "mywebsite" app by first opening the "/mywebsite/settings.py and executing the code below:

"#print "base dir path", BASE_DIR
#print os.path.join (os.path.dirname (BASE_DIR),
"mywebsite", "static", "templates")

TEMPLATE_DIRS = (
os.path.join(os.path.dirname (BASE_DIR), "mywebsite",
"static", "templates"),
#'/home/frankbox/python/djangoapp/mywebsite/static/te
mplates',
)"

The code above will define the directory of the templates being used. You can update the URL of your application form "mywebsite/mywebsite/urls.py" using the code below containing examples of potential new URLs:

"from django.conf.urls import patterns, include, url
from django.contrib import admin

urlpatterns = patterns ('',
 # Examples:
 # url (r'^$', 'mywebsite.views.home', name='home'),
 # url (r'^blog/', include ('blog.urls')),
url (r'^$', 'notes.views.home', name='home'),
url (r'^admin/', include (admin.site.urls)),
)"

You can create "/mywebsite/static/templates/" and add a simple static html file (note.html) to it. Then open the "/mywebsite/notes/views.py" and execute the code below:

"from django.shortcuts import render,
render_to_response, RequestContext
from django.template import RequestContext, loader
from django.http import HttpResponse

```
from .models import Note

# Required views can be created here.

def home (request):
notes = Note.objects
template = loader.get_template ('note.html')
context = {'notes': notes}
return render (request, 'note.html', context)
#return render_to_response ("note.html", notes)"
```

When the browser has been opened the list of all notes that you might have created will be displayed, as shown in the picture below:

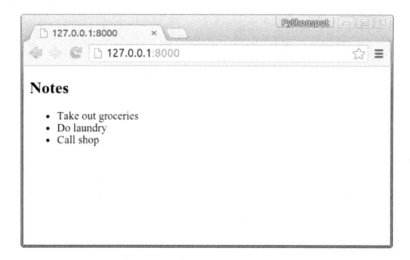

You will be able to **insert data** to the application by creating the "/mywebsite/notes/forms.py" file to use the code below:

```
"from django import forms
from .models import Note

class NoteForm (forms.ModelForm):
class Meta:
model = Note"
```

Then update the default view.py using the code below:

```
"from django.shortcuts import render,
render_to_response, RequestContext
from django.template import RequestContext, loader
from django.http import HttpResponse
from .models import Note
from .forms import NoteForm

# Create your views here.

def home(request):
notes = Note.objects
template = loader.get_template ('note.html')
form = NoteForm (request.POST or None)
```

```python
if form.is_valid ():
save_it = form.save (commit=False)
save_it.save ()


context = {'notes': notes, 'form': form}
return render (request, 'note.html', context)
#return render_to_response ("note.html", notes)"
```

Let's make the final updates to the notes.html file using the code below:

```
"<h2>Notes</h2>
<ul>
        & #123; % for note in notes.all %& #125;
        <li>& #123; & #123; note.text & #125; & #125;</li>
& #123;% endfor % & #125;</ul>
<form method = "POST" action= " "> & #123;%
csrf_token %& #125;
& #123; & #123; form.as_p & #125;& #125;
<input type = "submit">
</form>"
```

Now all you got to do is run your new notes taking application and you will see your browser appear as the picture shown below:

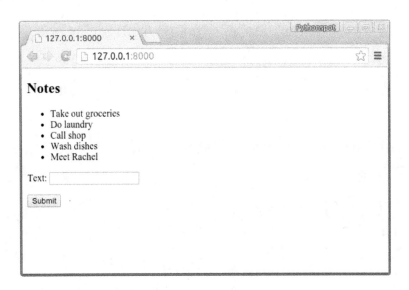

Lastly, you can also style your applications just like any other html/css websites by making desired changes to the "note.html" using the code below:

"*<link href =*
"http://codepen.io/edbond88/pen/CcgvA.css"
media="screen" rel= "stylesheet" type = "text/css">
<style>
        *body {
*
          *background: rgba (222,222,222,1);
*
          *margin: 20px;
*

```
}<br />
</style>
```

```
<h1>Django Note Taking App</h1>
```

```
<form method = "POST" action = ""> & #123; %
csrf_token % & #125;
{ { form.as_p }}
<input type = "submit" value = "Add note">
</form>"
```

Viola! Your notes taking application should look like the picture below:

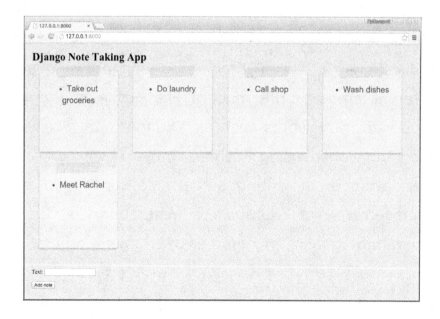

Day 7: Python Applications

Python is widely used for a large variety of web based projects spanning across the industrial spectrum. In the last chapter, you learned about the development of websites and web based applications using a Python based data framework. Python is widely used in the development and testing of software programs, machine learning algorithms and Artificial Intelligence technologies to solve real world problems. The science of developing human controlled and operated machinery, such as digital computers or robots, that can mimic human intelligence, adapt to new inputs and perform human like tasks is called "Artificial Intelligence" or AI. Let's look at real life applications of the Python programming language in different areas of the modern life. Some of the widely used web frameworks such as "Django" and "Flask" have been developed using Python. These frameworks assist the developer in writing server-side codes that enable management of database, generation of backend programming logic, mapping of URL, among others.

A variety of machine learning models have been written exclusively in Python. Machine learning is a way for machines to write logic in order to learn and fix a specific issue on its own. For instance, Python-based machine learning algorithms used in development of "product recommendation systems" for eCommerce businesses such as Amazon, Netflix, YouTube, and many more. Other instances of Python based machine learning models are the facial recognition and the voice recognition technologies available on our mobile devices. Python can also be used in the development of data visualization and data analysis tools and techniques such as scatter plots and other graphical representations of data.

"Scripting" can be defined as the process of generating simple programs for automation of straightforward tasks like those required to send automated email responses and text messages. You could develop these types of software using the Python programming language. A wide variety of gaming programs have been developed with the use of Python. Python also supports the development of "embedded applications". You could use data libraries such as "TKinter" or "QT" to create desktop apps based on Python.

Gaming Industry

Python based artificial intelligence programs are at the heart of the gaming industry, with its groundbreaking simulation and virtual experience technologies. In 1949, mathematician Claude Shannon developed a 'one player chess game' using the rudimentary Machine learning algorithms, where people would compete against a computer instead of another person. In 1989, the "Sim City" game successfully stimulated realistic and deeply human characteristics like unpredictability, with its use of artificial intelligence technology. In 2000, the "Total War" game incorporated human like emotions into their virtual fighters mimicking the soldiers in real-life battlefields.

In 2017, the leading gaming company, Electronic Arts, announced the establishment of their new research and development division called "SEED". This division is dedicated solely to exploration of artificial intelligence based technologies and creative opportunities for future giving products. Another billion-dollar gaming company called Epic Games collaborated with CubicMotion, 3Lateral, Tencent, and Vicon to develop in realistic virtual human named "Siren", marking a tremendous step forward in gaming as well as film industry.

Cost saving

Since the early 1980s, procedural content generation has become an area of grave importance for game development. This pertains to generation of game levels and rules, quest and stories, spatial maps, Music and props such as vehicles, weapons and powers as well as Game characters. This is gaming content creation; it's traditionally done by highly skilled Game artists and developers that tend to be expensive and in high demand. Development of a single game requires hundreds of people working for several years adding to the high cost of game development. Consequently, the gaming industry is enticed by the lucrative artificial intelligence technology to create high-quality gaming content at a faction of cost.

In 2018, Nivdia collaborated with an independent game development company called Remedy Entertainment to develop an automated real-time deep learning Technology that can create three-dimensional facial animations from audio. This technology will be useful in development of low cost localization, in-game dialogue and virtual reality avatars. In 2019, Italy's Politecnico di Milano launched a game level-design artificial intelligence using generative adversarial networks (GANs), which is a deep neutral network composed of two nets contested within each other. A popular first person shooter video game called "DOOM" now contains maps designed using this technology.

Enhancing gaming experience

The gaming industry is leveraging artificial intelligence Technology to understand what players do and how they feel during the play in order to be able to model a human player. To gauge and build models of player experience, supervised machine learning Technologies such as "Artificial Neural Networks" and "Support Vector Machines" are used. Select aspects of the game and player-game interaction serves as the training data resources. For example, the video game "Grand Theft Auto" is being used and the development off autonomous vehicles by training them to recognize stop signs. Another example of gaming technology being leveraged by AI researchers to aid in machine learning is the sandbox video game "Minecraft", which enables players to construct a virtual 3-D world using a variety of building blocks.

Automation and Personalization of customer service with Chatbots

With the advancements in the natural language processing technology, the consumers' ability to distinguish between the human voice and the voice of a robot is increasingly diminishing. Chatbots, with their more human like voices and ability to resolve customer issues independently and in the absence of human assistance is the future of customer service, and it's bound to expand from banking to all other industries. The banks will soon be reporting huge savings and significant cost reductions in the next 10 years. A recent study predicted up to $450 billion in savings by the banking and lending industry by 2030.

Despite this huge promise and reward brought on by AI powered Chatbots, banking and other industries need to tread with caution when it comes to delivering service that meets or succeeds customer expectations. The reality is humans today, and for the foreseeable future like to speak with another person to address and resolve their issues. The nuances of human problems seem too far-fetched to be understood by a callus robot. The best approach seems to be human customer service representatives augmented by the Chatbots rather than replacing humans completely. For example, the renowned Swiss bank UBS, with a global ranking of 35 for the volume of its assets, has partnered with Amazon. Amazon has successfully incorporated a "Ask UBS" service on their AI powered speakers called Amazon Echo (Alexa). UBS customers across the world can simply "ask" Alexa for advice and analysis on global financial markets in lieu of The Wall Street Journal. The "Ask UBS" service is also designed to offer definitions and examples for the finance related jargon and acronyms. However, "Ask UBS" application is unable to offer personalized advice to the UBS clients, owing to a lack of access to individual portfolios and client's holding and goals. This inability stems from security and privacy concerns regarding client data.

With the wealth of customer data including records of online and offline transactions and detailed demographics, banking industry is sitting on a gold mine that needs the power of AI based analytics to dig out the gold with data mining. Integration and analysis of information sourced from discrete databases has uniquely positioned banks to utilize Machine learning and obtain a complete view of their customers' needs and provide superior personalized services.

"The next step within the digital service model is for banks to price for the individual, and to negotiate that price in real time, taking personalization to the ultimate level".
– James Eardley, SAP Marketing Director

For all the financial institutions, customer personalization has transcended from marketing and product customization into the realm of cybersecurity. Biometric data, like fingerprints, is increasingly being used to augment or replace traditional passwords and other means of identity verification. A recent study by "Google Intelligence" reported that by 2021 about 2 billion bank customers would be using some or other form of biometric identification. One of the leading tech giants, Apple, has descended onto payment platform and is now using their Artificial Intelligence powered "facial recognition technology" to unlock their devices and also to validate payments, using their "digital wallet" service called "Apple Pay".

Healthcare Applications

- AI-assisted robotic surgery – The biggest draw of robot assisted surgery is that they do not require large incisions and are considered minimally invasive with low post-op recovery time. Robots are capable of analyzing data from pre-op patient medical records and subsequently guiding the surgeon's instruments during surgery. These robot-assisted surgeries have reported up to 21% reduction in patients' hospital stays. Robots can also use data from past surgeries and use AI to inform the surgeon about any new possible techniques. The most advanced surgical robot, "Da Vinci", allows surgeons to carry out complex surgical procedures with higher accuracy and greater control than the conventional methods.

- Supplement clinical diagnosis – Although the use of AI in diagnostics is still under the radar, a lot of successful use cases have already been reported. An algorithm created at Stanford University is capable of detecting skin cancer with similar competencies as that of a skilled dermatologist. An AI software program in Denmark was used to eavesdrop on emergency phone calls made to human dispatchers. The underlying algorithm analyzed the tone and words of the caller as well as the background noise to detect cases of heart attack. The AI program had a 93% success rate, which was 20% higher than the human counterparts.

- Virtual Nursing Assistants – The virtual nurses are available 24*7 without fatigue and lapse in judgment. They provide constant patient monitoring and directions for the most effective care while answering all of the patient's questions quickly and efficiently. An increase in regular communication between patients and their care providers can be credited to virtual nursing applications. This prevents unnecessary hospital visits and readmission. The virtual nurse assistant at Care Angel can already provide wellness checks through Artificial Intelligence and voice.

- Automation of administrative tasks – AI driven technology such as voice to text transcriptions are aiding in ordering test, prescribing medications, and even writing medical chart notes. The partnership between IBM and Cleveland Clinic has allowed IBM's Watson to perform mining on clinical health data and help physicians in developing personalized and more efficient treatment plans.

Finance Sector

Fraud Prevention

The inherent capability of Artificial Intelligence to swiftly analyze large volumes of data and identify patterns that may not come naturally to the human observer has made AI the smoking gun for fraud detection and prevention. According to a recent report by McAfee global economy suffered a $600 billion loss through cybercrime alone. Real time fraud detection is the only direct path to prevent fraud from happening in the first place.

AI and machine learning based solutions are empowering financial service providers with real time fraud detection as well reducing the frequency of legitimate transactions being flagged as fraudulent. The MasterCard company has reported an 80% decline in legitimate activity being marked as "false fraud", with its use of Artificial Intelligence technology.

Lending risk management

Banks and other money lending institutions bear high risk while giving out loans to the borrowers. This complex process of underwriting requires accuracy and high confidentiality. This is where AI swoops in to save the day by analyzing available transaction data, market trends, and recent financial activities pertinent to the prospective borrower and assessing potential risks in approving the loan(s).

Hedge Fund Management

Today, over $3 trillion in assets of the world economy are managed by hedge funds. The investment partnerships between investors or "limited partners" and professional fund managers are called hedge funds. Hedge fund's strategy to minimize the risk and maximize returns for the investors dictates the contribution made by the "limited partner" and the management of those funds by the general partner. The hedge funds epitomize the idiom "bigger the risk, bigger the reward" and are considered riskier investments. The hedge fund managers are responsible for shorting their stocks if they anticipate the market will drop or "hedge" by going long when they anticipate the market will grow. This stock trading can soon be taken over Artificial Intelligence based solutions requiring no human intervention and revolutionize the hedge fund management.

The ability of Artificial Intelligence powered machines to analyze massive amounts of data in fraction of time; then, it takes a human and gather insight from its analysis to self-learn and improve its trading acumen is indeed a big winner. As intriguing as the use of AI to trade stocks appears, it is still missing the proof of concept but nevertheless, companies are continuing to research and develop AI powered systems that could potentially kick start a new era on Wall Street.

Transportation Industry

The transportation industry is highly susceptible two problems arising from human errors, traffic, and for accidents. These problems are too difficult to model owing to their inherently unpredictable nature but can be easily overcome with the use of Artificial Intelligence powered tools that can analyze observed data and make or predict the appropriate decisions. The challenge of increasing travel demand, safety concerns, CO2 emissions and environmental degradation can be met with the power of artificial intelligence. From Artificial Neural Networks to Bee colony optimization, a whole lot of artificial intelligence techniques are being employed to make transportation industry efficient and effective. To obtain significant relief from traffic congestion while making travel time more reliable for the population, transport authorities are experimenting with a variety of AI based solutions. With potential application of artificial intelligence for enhanced road infrastructure and assistance for drivers, transportation industry it's focused on accomplishing a more reliable transport system, which will have limited to no effect on the environment while being cost effective.

It is an uphill battle to fully understand the relationships between the characteristics of various transportation systems using the traditional methods. Artificial intelligence is here once again to offer the panacea by transforming the traffic sensors on the road into a smart agent that can potentially detect accidents and predict the future traffic conditions. Rapid development has been observed in the area of Intelligent Transport Systems (ITS), which are targeted to alleviate traffic congestion and improve driving experience by utilizing multiple Technologies and communication systems. They are capable of collecting and storing data that can be easily integrated with machine learning technology. To increase the efficiency of police patrol and keeping the citizens of safe collection of crime data is critical and can be achieved with right AI powered tools. Artificial intelligence can also simplify the transportation planning of the road freight transport system by providing accurate prediction methods to forecast their volume.

Here are some real world examples of artificial intelligence being used in the transportation industry:

- Local motors company, in collaboration with IBM's Watson has unveiled an AI powered autonomous fully electric vehicle called "Olli".
- A highly promising traffic control system developed by Rapid Flow Technologies is called "SURTRAC", which allows traffic lights at intersections to respond to vehicular flow on an individual level instead of being a part of a centralized system.

A Chinese company called "TuSimple" entered American market with their self-driving trucks that can utilize long distance sensors with a complete observation range and it's deep learning artificial intelligence technology allows seamless detection and tracking of objects using multiple cameras.

- Rolls-Royce is expected to launch air own clueless cargo ships by 2020 that could be controlled remotely and pioneer the way for fully autonomous ships in near future.

In early 2019, the first autonomous trains were tested by the London underground train system that can potentially carry more passengers in lieu of driver's cabin.

- Some commuters in Sweden have reportedly been testing microchip implants on their body as travel tickets.

- China launched the Autonomous Rail Rapid Transit System (ART) in the city of Zhuzhou that doesn't require tracks, and instead, the trains follow of virtual track created by painted dashed lines.

Autonomous delivery trucks could soon be bringing our food and mail to us instead of the human driven delivery service.

- Dubai is experimenting with Smart technology driven digital number plates for cars, which can immediately send an alert to the authorities in the event of an accident.

• Some of the American airports are you using artificial intelligence a face scanning technologies to verify the identities of passengers before allowing them to board the flight and ditching the traditional passports.

• The revolutionizing Google flights technology is able to predict flight delays before the airlines themselves by using Advanced machine learning technology on the available data from previous flights and providing passengers a more accurate expected time of arrival.

• When it comes to real-time customer service, the Trainline app has surpassed all AI powered applications on the market, with its BusyBot technology that can help the passengers with there change tickets booking and purchase as well as find a vacant seat on the train in real-time. This bot collects information from the passengers onboard on how busy their carriages are and then analyzes that data to advise other passengers on potentially vacant seating.

- The "JOZU" app is aimed at once again liberating the modern woman who likes to travel alone and is concerned about her safety. It collects user data to provide women with the safest routes and methods of transport.

- China has pioneered the development of smart highway that can charge electric vehicles as they are driving, and Australia is set to follow the lead. Smart roads are being designed to incorporate sensors to monitor traffic patterns and solar panels for vehicle charging.

- Smart luggage with built-in GPS tracker and weighing scales connected to your phones are already available on the market.

- Ford has recently announced its plan to file a patent for their Artificial Intelligence based unmanned "Robotic Police Car" that can issue tickets for speeding and other violations to drivers by scanning their car registration and accessing the CCTV footage.

- Japan will soon be enjoying a new ride-hailing service. Sony recently announced launch of their new service that will use Artificial Intelligence to manage fleets and provide an overview of potential traffic issues like congestions and detours due to public events.

- Ford has designed a "Smart City" with the system that allows smart vehicles to connect and coordinate with one another while cutting down on the risks of collisions and other accidents. The Smart city would collect data from its residents and share it with multiple smart technologies working in tandem to create a digital utopia.

Tips and Tricks for Developers

Here are some of the tips and tricks you can leverage to sharpen up your Python programming skill set are:

In-place swapping of two numbers:

```
x, y = 102, 202
print (x, y)
x, y = y, x
print (x, y)"
```

Resulting Output =
102 202
202 102

Reversing a string:

```
x ="christmas"
print ("Reverse is", x [::-1])
```

Resulting Output =
Reverse is samtsirhc.

Creating a single string from multiple list elements:

```
x = ["have", "a", "happy"",new", "year"]
print (" ".join (x))
```

Resulting Output =
have a happy new year

Stacking of comparison operators:
```
n = 102
result = 1 < n < 202
print (result)
result = 1 > n <= 92
print (result)
```

Resulting Output =
True
False

Print the file path of the imported modules:
```
import os;
import socket;
  print(os)
print (socket
```

Resulting Output =

"<module 'os' from '/usr/lib/python3.5/os.py'>

<module 'socket' from '/usr/lib/python3.5/socket.py'>"

Use of enums in Python:

class MyName:

   Eye, For, Eye= range (3)

print (MyName.Eye)

print (MyName.For)

print (MyName.Eye)

Resulting Output =

2

1

2

Result in multiple values from functions:

def x ():

   result in 12, 22, 32, 42

a, b, c, d = x ()

print (a, b, c, d)

Resulting Output =

12 22 32 42

Identify the value with highest frequency:

test = [11, 21, 31, 41, 21, 21, 31, 11, 41, 41, 41]

print (max(set(test), key = test.count))

Resulting Output =

41

Check the memory usage of an object:

import sys

x = 1

print (sys.getsizeof (x))

Resulting Output =

28

Printing a string N times:

n = 3;

a ="PythonCoding";

print (a * n);

Resulting Output =

PythonCodingPythonCodingPythonCoding

Identify anagrams:

from collections import Counter

```python
def is_anagram (str1, str2):
    result in Counter(str1) == Counter(str2)
print (is_anagram ('home', 'emoh'))

print (is_anagram ('home', 'rome'))
```

Resulting Output =
True
False

Transposing a matrix:

```python
mat = [[12, 22, 32], [42, 52, 62]]
zip (*mat)
```

Resulting Output =
[(12, 42), (22, 52), (32, 62)]

Print a repeated string without using loops:

```python
print "Python"*3+' '+"Programming"*2
```
Resulting Output =
PythonPythonPython ProgrammingProgramming

Measure the code execution time:

```python
import time
```

```
startTime = time.time()
"write your code or functions calls"
"write your code or functions calls"
endTime = time.time ()
totalTime = endTime – startTime
print ('Total time required to execute code is=' ,
totalTime)
```

Resulting Output =
Total time

Obtain the difference between two lists:
```
list1 = ['Ryan', 'Prim', 'Keith', 'Dan', 'Sam']
list2 = ['Sam', 'Dan', 'Keith']
set1 = set(list1)
set2 = set(list2)
list3 = list(set1.symmetric_difference(set2))
print(list3)
```
Resulting Output =
list3 = ['Ryan', 'Prim']

Calculate the memory being used by an object in Python:
```
import sys
```

```
list1 = ['Ryan', 'Prim', 'Keith', 'Dan', 'Sam']
print ("size of list = ", sys.getsizeof(list1))
name = 'pynative.com'
print ('size of name =', sys.getsizeof(name))
```

Resulting Output =
('size of list = ', 112)
('size of name = ', 49)

Removing duplicate items from the list:

```
listNumbers = [40, 44, 44, 46, 48, 48, 40, 30, 44]
print ('Original=' , listNumbers)
listNumbers = list(set(listNumbers))
print ('After removing duplicate= ' , listNumbers)
```

Resulting Output =
'Original= ', [40, 44, 44, 46, 48, 48, 40, 30, 44]
'After removing duplicate= ', [40, 44, 44, 46, 48, 30]

Find if a list contains identical elements:

```
listOne = [18, 18, 18, 18]
print ('All elements are duplicate in listOne',
listOne.count(listOne[0]) == len(listOne))
listTwo = [18, 18, 18, 50]
```

print ('All elements are duplicate in listTwo',
listTwo.count(listTwo[0]) == len(listTwo))

Resulting Output =

"'All elements are duplicate in listOne', True"

"'All elements are duplicate in listTwo', False"

Efficiently compare two unordered lists:

from collections import Counter

one = [33, 22, 11, 44, 55]

two = [22, 11, 44, 55, 33]

*print ('is two list are b equal', Counter(one) ==
Counter(two))*

Resulting Output =

"'is two list are b equal', True"

Check if list contains all unique elements:

def isUnique(item):

tempSet = set ()

*result in not any (i in tempSet or tempSet.add(i) for i in
item)*

listOne = [123, 345, 456, 23, 567]

print ('All List elements are Unique' , isUnique(listOne))

listTwo = [123, 345, 567, 23, 567]

print ('All List elements are Unique' , isUnique(listTwo))

Resulting Output =

"All List elements are Unique True"

"All List elements are Unique False"

Convert Byte into String:

byteVar = b"pynative"

str = str (byteVar.decode ('utf-8'))

print ('Byte to string is', str)

Resulting Output =

"Byte to string is pynative"

Merge two dictionaries into a single expression:

currentEmployee = {1: 'Scott', 2: 'Eric', 3:'Kelly'}

formerEmployee = {2: 'Eric', 4: 'Emma'}

def merge_dicts(dictOne, dictTwo):

dictThree = dictOne.copy()

dictThree.update(dictTwo)

result in dictThree

print (merge_dicts (currentEmployee,

formerEmployee))

Extra content

Python programming: An hands-on introduction to computer programming and algorithms, a project-based guide with practical exercises (Book 1) has been structured as a 7-day-course with seven chapter (one per day), to guide the reader in a journey into the huge worl of Python.

The journey is thought and structured by Computer Programming Academy as a month long course. So it is just began!

This book is part of a series with other two:
- *Python Machine Learning: An hands-on introduction to artificial intelligence coding, a project-based guide with practical exercises (Book 2)*
- *Python Data Science: An hands-on introduction to big data analysis and data mining, a project-based guide with practical exercises (Book 3)*

Here below a free sneak peak of Book *2 Python Machine Learning* and Book 3 **Python Data Science,** enjoy!

Python Machine Learning: An hands-on introduction to artificial intelligence coding, a project-based guide with practical exercises (Book 2)

This book will discuss the fundamental concepts of machine learning models that can be generated and advanced by utilizing Python based libraries.

The first chapter will introduce you to the core concepts of machine learning as well as various terminologies that are frequently used in this field. It will also provide you a thorough understanding of the significance of machine learning in our daily lives. Some of the most widely used learning models, such as Artificial Neural Networks (ANN) and Genetic Algorithms (GA) are explained in detail in the second chapter.

Chapter 3 will introduce you to the four fundamental machine learning algorithms with explicit details on the supervised machine learning algorithms. The subsequent chapter will include details on various unsupervised machine learning algorithms, such as clustering and dimensionality reduction among others.

You will also learn how the raw data can be processed to generate high quality training data set for the production of a successful machine learning model. The sixth chapter of this book will deep dive into the functioning of ML library called Scikit-Learn along with guidance on resolving nonlinear issues with k-nearest neighbor and kernel trick algorithms. The final chapter will explain the nuances of developing a neural network to generate predictions and build the desired machine learning model by utilizing the Tensorflow Python library.

We have also provided review exercises to help you test your understanding through this process. Every chapter of this book has real life examples and applications included to solidify your understanding of each concept.

Day 1: Introduction to Machine Learning

The modern concept of Artificial Intelligence technology is derived from the idea that machines are capable of human like intelligence and potentially mimic human thought processing and learning capabilities to adapt to fresh inputs and perform tasks with no human assistance. Machine learning is integral to the concept of artificial intelligence. Machine Learning can be defined as a concept of Artificial Intelligence technology that focuses primarily on the engineered capability of machines to explicitly learn and self-train, by identifying data patterns to improve upon the underlying algorithm and make independent decisions with no human intervention. In 1959, pioneering computer gaming and artificial intelligence expert, Arthur Samuel, coined the term "machine learning" during his tenure at IBM.

Machine learning stems from the hypothesis that modern day computers have an ability to be trained by utilizing targeted training data sets, that can be easily customized to develop desired functionalities. Machine learning is driven by the pattern recognition technique wherein the machine records and revisits past interactions and results that are deemed in alignment with its current situation. Given the fact that machines are required to process endless amounts of data, with new data always pouring in, they must be equipped to adapt to the new data without needing to be programmed by a human, which speaks to the iterative aspect of machine learning.

Now the topic of machine learning is so "hot" that the world of academia, business as well as the scientific community have their own take on its definition. Here are a few of the widely accepted definitions from select highly reputed sources:

- *"Machine learning is the science of getting computers to act without being explicitly programmed". –* Stanford University
- *"The field of Machine Learning seeks to answer the question, "How can we build computer systems that automatically improve with experience, and what are the fundamental laws that govern all learning processes?" –* Carnegie Mellon University
- *"Machine learning algorithms can figure out how to perform important tasks by generalizing from examples". –* University of Washington
- *"Machine Learning, at its most basic, is the practice of using algorithms to parse data, learn from it, and then make a determination or prediction about something in the world". –* Nvidia

- *"Machine learning is based on algorithms that can learn from data without relying on rules-based programming".* – McKinsey & Co.

Core concepts of machine learning

The biggest draw of this technology is its inherent ability of the system to automatically learn programs from the raw data in lieu of manually engineering the program for the machine. Over the last 10 years or so, the application of ML algorithms has expanded from computer science labs to the industrial world. Machine learning algorithms are capable of generalizing tasks so they can be executed iteratively.

The process of developing specific programs for specific tasks is extremely taxing in terms of time and money, but occasionally, it is just impossible to achieve. On the other hand, machine learning programming is often feasible and tends to be much more cost effective. The use of machine learning in addressing ambitious issues of widespread importance such as global warming and depleting underground water levels, is promising with massive collection of relevant data.

"A breakthrough in machine learning would be worth ten Microsofts".

– Bill Gates

A number of different types of ML models exist today, but the concept of ML largely boils down to three core components "representation", "evaluation", and "optimization". Here are some of the standard concepts that are applicable to all of them:

Representation

Machine learning models are incapable of directly hearing, seeing, or sensing input examples. Therefore, data representation is required to supply the model with a useful vantage point into the key qualities of the data. To be able to successfully train a machine learning model selection of key features that best represent the data is very important. "Representation" simply refers to the act of representing data points to the computing system in a language that it understands with the use of a set of classifiers. A classifier can be defined as "a system that inputs a vector of discrete and or continuous feature values and outputs a single discrete value called class". For a model to learn from the represented data, the

216

training data set or the "hypothesis space" must contain the desired classifier that you want the models to be trained on. Any classifiers that are external to the hypothesis space cannot be learned by the model. The data features used to represent the input are extremely crucial to the machine learning process. The data features are so critical to the development of the desired machine learning model that it could easily be the key distinction between a successful and failed machine learning project. A training data set consisting of multiple independent feature sets that are well correlated with the class can make the machine learning much smoother. On the other hand, class consisting of complex features may not be easy to learn from for the machine. This usually needs the raw data to be processed to allow the construction of desired features from it, which could then be utilized for the development of the ML model. The process of deriving features from raw data tends to be the most time consuming and laborious part of the ML projects. It is also considered the most creative and exciting part of the project where intuition and trial and error play just as important role as the technical requirements. The process of ML is not a single shot process of developing a training data set and executing it; instead, it's an iterative process that requires analysis of the post run results followed by modification of the training data set and then repeating the whole process all over again. Another contributing factor to the extensive time and effort required in the engineering of the training data set is domain specificity. Training data set for an e-commerce platform to generate predictions based on consumer behavior analysis will be very different from the training data set required to develop a self-driving car. However, the actual machine learning process largely holds true across the industrial spectrum. No wonder, a lot of research is being done to automate the feature engineering process.

Evaluation

Essentially the process of judging multiple hypothesis or models to choose one model over another is referred to as an evaluation. To be able to differentiate between good classifiers from the not so good ones, an "evaluation function" must be used. The evaluation function is also called "objective", "utility", or "scoring" function. The machine learning algorithm has its own internal evaluation function, which tends to be different from the external evaluation function used by the researchers to optimize the classifier. Normally the evaluation function will be defined prior to the selection of the data representation tool and tends to be the first step of the project. For example, the machine learning model for self-driving cars has a feature that allows identification of pedestrians in the car's vicinity at near zero false negatives and a low false positive, which are the evaluation functions and the pre-existing condition that needs to be "represented" using applicable data features.

Optimization

The process of searching the space of presented models to achieve better evaluations or highest scoring classifier is called as "optimization". For algorithms with multiple optimum classifiers, the selection of optimization technique is very important in the determination of the classifier produced as well as to achieve a more efficient learning model. A variety of off-the-shelf optimizers are available in the market that will help you kick start a new machine learning model before eventually replacing them with a custom designed optimizers.

Basic machine learning terminologies

Agent – In context of reinforcement learning, an agent refers to an entity that utilizes a policy to max out the expected return achieved with the transition of different environment states.

Boosting – Boosting can be defined as a ML technique that would sequentially combine set of simple and low accuracy classifiers (known as "weak" classifiers) into a classifier which is highly accurate (known as "strong" classifier) by increasing the weight of the samples that are being classified wrongly by the model.

Candidate generation – The phase of selecting the initial set of suggestions provided by a recommendation system is referred to as candidate generation. For example, a book library can offer 60,000 different books. Through this phase, a subset of few 100 titles meeting the needs of a particular user will be produced and can be refined further to an even smaller set as needed.

Categorical Data – Data features boasting a distinct set of potential values is called as categorical data. For example, a categorical feature named TV model can have a discrete set of multiple possible values, including Smart, Roku, Fire.

Checkpoint – Checkpoint can be defined as a data point that will capture the state of the variables at a specific moment in time of the ML model. With the use of checkpoints, training can be carried out across multiple sessions and model weights or scores can be exported.

Class – Class can be defined as "one of a set of listed target values for a given label". For instance, a model designed to detect junk emails can have 2 different classes, namely, "spam" and "not spam".

Classification model – The type of machine learning model used to differentiate between multiple distinct classes of the data is referred to as a classification model. For example, a classification model for identification of dog breeds could assess whether the dog picture used as input is Labrador, Schnauzer, German Shepherd, Beagle and so on.

Collaborative filtering – The process of generating predictions for a particular user based on the shared interests of a group of similar users is called collaborative filtering.

Continuous feature – It is defined as a "floating point feature with an infinite range of possible values".

Discrete feature – It is defined as a feature that can be given only a finite set of potential values and has no flexibility.

Discriminator – A system used to determine whether the input samples are realistic or not is called as discriminator.

Down-sampling – The process of Down-sampling refers to the process used to reduce the amount of info comprised in a feature or use of an extremely low percentage of classes that are abundantly represented in order to train the ML model with higher efficiency.

Dynamic model – A learning model that is continuously receiving input data to be trained in a continuous manner is called a dynamic model.

Ensemble – A set of predictions created by combining predictions of more than one model is called an ensemble.

Environment – The term environment used in the context of reinforcement machine learning constitutes "the world that contains the agent and allows the agent to observe that world's state".

Episode – The term episode used in the context of reinforcement machine learning constitutes every sequential trial taken by the model to learn from its environment.

Feature – Any of the data variables that can be used as an input to generate predictions is called a feature.

Feature engineering – Feature engineering can be defined as "the process of determining which features might be useful in training a model, and then converting raw data from log files and other sources into said features".

Feature extraction – Feature extraction can be defined as "the process of retrieving intermediate feature representations calculated by an unsupervised or pre-trained model for use in another model as input".

Few-shot learning - Few-shot learning can be defined as "a machine learning approach, often used for object classification, designed to learn effective classifiers from only a small number of training examples".

Fine tuning – The process of "performing a secondary optimization to adjust the parameters of an already trained model to fit a new problem" is called as fine tuning. It is widely used to refit the weight(s) of a "trained unsupervised model" to a "supervised model".

Generalization – A machine learning model's capability to produce accurate predictions from fresh and unknown input data instead of the data set utilized during the training phase of the model is called generalization.

Inference – In context of ML, inference pertains to the process of generating predictions and insight with the application of an already trained model to unorganized data sample.

Label – In context of machine learning (supervised), the "answer" or "result" part of an example is called a label. Each title in a labeled dataset will consist of single or multiple features along with a label. For example, in a house data set, the features could contain the year built, number of rooms and bathrooms, while the label can be the "house's price".

Linear model – Linear model is defined as a model that can assign singular weight to each feature for generating predictions.

Loss – In context of ML, loss pertains to the measure of the extent by which the predictions produced by the model are not in line with its training labels.

Matplotlib – It is an "open source Python 2-D plotting library" that can be utilized to visualize various elements of ML.

Model – In context of ML, a model refers to a representation of the learning and training that has been acquired by the system from the training dataset.

NumPy – It is an open sourced data library that can provide effective operations to be used on Python arrays.

One-shot learning – In context of machine learning, one-shot learning can be defined as the machine learning approach that allows learning of effective classifiers from unique training sample and is frequently utilized classification of objects.

Overfitting - In context of machine learning, overfitting is referred to as production of a model that can match the training dataset extremely closely and renders the model inefficient in making accurate predictions on fresh input.

Parameter – Any variable of the ML model, which would allow the machine learning system to self-learn independently is called parameter.

Pipeline – In context of ML, pipeline pertains to the infrastructure that surrounds a learning algorithm and comprises of a collection of data, any data additions made to the training data files, training of single or multiple models, and releasing the models into live environment.

Random forest – In context of machine learning, the concept of random forest pertains to an ensemble technique to find a decision tree that would most accurately fit the training dataset by creating two or more decision trees with a random selection of features.

Scaling - In context of machine learning, scaling refers to "a common feature engineering practice to tame a feature's range of values to match the range of other features in the dataset".

Sequence model - A sequence model simply refers to a model with sequential dependency on data inputs to generate a future prediction.

Underfitting – It is the process of generating a model with low efficacy to generate predictions due to the lack of proper understanding of the training data set.

Python Data Science: An hands-on introduction to big data analysis and data mining, a project-based guide with practical exercises (Book 3)

This book will discuss the fundamental concepts of data science technologies that can be used to analyze raw data and generate predictions and resolve business problems.

The first chapter of the book will help you understand the importance of data science technologies in our everyday lives ranging from weather forecasting to cyber attacks. You will also learn different types of data and various data science implementation strategies. A detailed overview of the "Team Data Science Process", which is a data science lifecycle widely used for projects that require the deployment of applications based on artificial intelligence and/or machine learning algorithms, has been provided in the second chapter. You will learn the objectives defined at each of the 5 stages of this lifecycle along with the deliverables that are created at the end of each stage.

The third chapter is all about big data and big data analytics. You will learn the 5 Vs of big data and the 3 important actions required to gain insights from big data. You will also learn the different steps involved in big data analysis and some of its applications in healthcare, finance, and other industrial sectors. The chapter entitled "Basics of Data Mining" will provide an explicit overview of the data mining process and its applications. You will also learn the advantages and challenge of the data mining process in resolving real world data problems. Some of the most widely used data mining tools that are being used by data analysts are also explained.

The fifth chapter deals exclusively with some of the key data analysis frameworks, including ensemble learning, decision trees and random forests. These are the most popular machine learning algorithms that are capable of processing a large volume of unstructured and unorganized data to generate useful insights and predictions. You will learn the advantages and disadvantages of these frameworks as well as the steps required to implement random forest regression on a real life dataset. Chapter six, entitled "Data Analysis Libraries", is a deep dive into the functioning of different Python based data analysis libraries including IPython, Jupyter Notebook, Pandas, Matplotlib among others. You will learn how these powerful libraries can be used to analyze real life data set with select open source sample dataset that you can download and gain hands-on experience with.

The final chapter of this book will explain to you how the data analysis helps resolve business issues using customer and/or predictive analytics. Customer analytics is at the heart of all marketing activities and is an umbrella term used for techniques such as "predictive modeling", "data visualization", "information management", and "segmentation". You will learn the important concept of marketing and sales funnel analytics as well as the three main types of predictive models to analyze customer behavior. The concepts of exploratory analysis of customer data and personalized marketing have been explained in detail, along with some of their industrial applications. To make the best use of this book, I recommend that you download the free resources provided in this book and perform hands-on exercises to solidify your understanding of the concepts explained. The skillset of data analysis is always in demand, with a lot of high pay job opportunities. Here's hoping this book has taken you a step closer to your dream job!

We have also provided review exercises to help you test your understanding through this process. Every chapter of this book has real life examples and applications included to solidify your understanding of each concept.

Day 1: Introduction to Data Science

In the world of technology, Data is defined as "information that is processed and stored by a computer". Our digital world has flooded our realities with data. From a click on a website to our smart phones tracking and recording our location every second of the day, our world is drowning in the data. From the depth of this humongous data, solutions to our problems that we have not even encountered yet could be extracted. This very process of gathering insights from a measurable set of data using mathematical equations and statistics can be defined as "data science". The role of data scientists tends to be very versatile and is often confused with a computer scientist and a statistician. Essentially anyone, be it a person or a company that is willing to dig deep to large volumes of data to gather information, can be referred to us data science practitioners. For example, companies like Walmart keeps track of and record of in-store and online purchases made by the customers, to provide personalized recommendations on products and services. The social media platforms like Facebook that allow users to list their current location is capable of identifying global migration patterns by analyzing the wealth of data that is handed to them by the users themselves.

The earliest recorded use of the term data science goes back to 1960 and credited to Pete Naur, who reportedly used the term data science as a substitute for computer science and eventually introduced the term "datalogy". In 1974, Naur published a book titled "Concise Survey of Computer Methods", with liberal use of the term data science throughout the book. In 1992, the contemporary definition of data science was proposed at "The Second Japanese-French Statistics Symposium", with the acknowledgment of emergence of a new discipline focused primarily on types, dimensions and structures of data.

"Data science continues to evolve as one of the most promising and in-demand career paths for skilled professionals. Today, successful data professionals

understand that they must advance past the traditional skills of analyzing large amounts of data, data mining, and programming skills. In order to uncover useful intelligence for their organizations, data scientists must master the full spectrum of the data science life cycle and possess a level of flexibility and understanding to maximize returns at each phase of the process".

– University of California, Berkley

An increasing interest by business executives has significantly contributed to the recent rise in popularity of the term data science. However, a large number of journalists and academic experts, do not acknowledge data science as a separate area of study from the field of statistics. A group within the same community considers data science is the popular term for "data mining" and "big data". The very definition of data science is up for debate within the tech community. The field of study that requires a combination of skill set including computer programming skills, domain expertise and proficiency in statistics and mathematical algorithms to be able to extract valuable insight from large volumes of raw data is referred to as data science.

Importance of Data Science

Data Science is heavily used in Predictive analysis. For example, weather forecast requires collection and analysis of data from a variety of sources, including satellites, radars, and aircraft, to build data models that are even capable of predicting the occurrence of catastrophes of the nature such as hurricanes, tornadoes and flash floods. Another branch of data science is "big data and big data analytics", which are used by organizations to address complex technical problems as well as for resource management. You will learn more about big data later in this book. The ability of data science to analyze the challenges facing any and all industrial sectors like healthcare, travel, finance, retail, and e-commerce has contributed significantly to its increasing popularity among business executives.Data science has made the use of advanced machine learning algorithms possible, which has a wide variety of applicability across multiple industrial domains. For example, the development of self-driving cars that are capable of collecting real-time data using their advanced cameras and sensors to create a map of their surroundings and make decisions pertaining to the speed of the vehicle and other driving maneuvers. Companies are always on the prowl to better understand the need of their customers. This is now achievable by gathering the data from existing sources like customer's order history, recently viewed items, gender, age and demographics and applying advanced analytical tools and algorithms over this data to gain valuable insights. With the use of machine learning algorithms, the system can generate product recommendations for individual customers with higher accuracy. The smart consumer is always looking for the most engaging and enhanced user experience, so the companies can use these analytical tools and algorithms to gain a competitive edge and grow their business.

The ability to analyze and closely examine Data trends and patterns using Machine learning algorithms has resulted in the significant application of data science in the cybersecurity space. With the use of data science, companies are not only able to identify the specific network terminal(s) that initiated the cyber attack but are also in a position to predict potential future attacks on their systems and take required measures to prevent the attacks from happening in the first place. The use of "active intrusion detection systems" that are capable of monitoring users and devices on any network of choice and flag any unusual activity serves as a powerful weapon against hackers and cyber attackers. While the "predictive intrusion detection systems" that are capable of using machine learning algorithms on historical data to detect potential security threats serves as a powerful shield against the cyber predators. Cyber attacks can result in a loss of priceless data and information resulting in extreme damage to the organization. To secure and protect the data set, sophisticated encryption and complex signatures can be used to prevent unauthorized access. Data science can help with the development of such impenetrable protocols and algorithms. By analyzing the trends and patterns of previous cyber attacks on companies across different industrial sectors, Data science can help detect the most frequently targeted data set and even predict potential future cyber attacks. Companies rely heavily on the data generated and authorized by their customers but in the light of increasing cyber attacks, customers are extremely wary of their personal information being compromised and are looking to take their businesses to the companies that are able to assure them of their data security and privacy by implementing advanced data security tools and technologies. This is where data science is becoming the saving grace of the companies by helping them enhance their cybersecurity measures.

Over the course of the past 20 years, Data trends have drastically changed, signaling an ongoing increase in unstructured data. It is estimated that by the year 2020, "more than 80% of the data that we gather will be unstructured". Conventionally, the data that we procured was primarily structured and could be easily analyzed using simple business intelligence tools but as reflected in the picture below unstructured and semi-structured data is on the rise. This, in turn, has warranted the development and use of more powerful and advanced analytical tools than the existing business intelligence tools that are incapable of processing such large volume and variety of data.

Types of Data

Let us look at different types of data so you can choose the most appropriate analytical tools and algorithms based on the type of data that needs to be processed. Data types can be divided into two at a very high level: qualitative and quantitative.

Qualitative data – Any data that cannot be measured and only observed subjectively by adding a qualitative feature to the object it's called as "qualitative data". Classification of an object using unmeasurable features results in the creation of qualitative data. For example, attributes like color, smell, texture, and taste. There are three types of qualitative data:

- **"Binary or binomial data"** – Data values that signal mutually exclusive events where only one of the two categories or options is correct and applicable. For example, true or false, yes or no, positive or negative. Consider a box of assorted tea bags. You try all the different flavors and group the ones that you like as "good" and the ones you don't as "bad". In this case, "good or bad" would be categorized as the binomial data type. This type of data is widely used in the development of statistical models for predictive analysis.

- **"Nominal or unordered data"** – Data characteristics that lack an "implicit or natural value" can be referred to as nominal data. Consider a box of M&Ms, you can record the color of each

M&M in the box in a worksheet, and that would serve as nominal data. This kind of data is widely used to assess statistical differences in the data set, using techniques like "Chi-Square analysis", which could tell you "statistically significant differences" in the amount of each color of M&M in a box.

- **"Ordered or ordinal data"** – The characteristics of this Data type do have certain "implicit or natural of value" such as small, medium, or large. For example, online reviews on sites like "Yelp", "Amazon", and "Trip Advisor" have a rating scale from 1 to 5, implying a 5-star rating is better than 4 which is better than 3 and so on.

Quantitative data – Any characteristics of the data that can be measured objectively are called as "quantitative data". Classification of an object in using measurable features and giving it a numerical value results and creation of quantitative data. For example, product prices, temperature, dimensions like length, etc. There are two types of quantitative data:

"Continuous Data" – Data values that can be defined to a further lower level, such as units of measurement like kilometers, meters, centimeters, and on and on, are called the continuous data type. For example, you can purchase a bag of almonds by weight like 500 g or 8 ounces. This accounts for the continuous data type, which is primarily used to test and verify different kinds of hypotheses such as assessing the accuracy of the weight printed on the bag of almonds.

- **"Discrete Data"** – numerical data value that cannot be divided and reduced to a higher level of precision, such as the number of cars owned by a person which can only be accounted for as indivisible numbers (you cannot have 1.5 or 2.3 cars), is called as discrete data types. For example, you can purchase another bag of ice cream bars by the number of ice cream bars inside the package, like four or six. This accounts for the discrete data type, which can be used in combination with a continuous data type to perform a regression analysis to verify if the total weight of the ice cream box (continuous data) is correlated with the number of ice cream bars (discrete data) inside.

Data science strategies

Data science is mainly used in decision-making by making precise predictions with the use of "predictive causal analytics", "prescriptive analytics", and machine learning.

Predictive causal analytics –"predictive causal analytics" can be applied to develop a model that can accurately predict and forecast the likelihood of a particular event occurring in the future. For example, financial institutions use predictive causal analytics based tools to assess the likelihood of a customer defaulting on their credit card payments, by generating a model that can analyze the payment history of the customer with all of their borrowing institutions.

Prescriptive analytics - The "prescriptive analytics" are widely used in the development of "intelligent tools and applications" that are capable of modifying and learning with dynamic parameters and make their own "decisions". The tool not only predicts the occurrence of a future event but is also capable of providing recommendations on a variety of actions and its resulting outcomes. For example, the self driving cars gather driving related data with every driving experience and use it to train themselves to make better driving and maneuvering decisions.

Machine learning to make predictions – To develop models that can determine future trends based on the transactional data acquired by the company, machine learning algorithms are a necessity. This is considered as "supervised machine learning", which we will elaborate on later in this book. For example, fraud detection systems use machine learning algorithms on the historical data pertaining to fraudulent purchases to detect if a transaction is fraudulent.

Machine learning for pattern discovery – To be able to develop models that are capable of identifying hidden data patterns but lack required parameters to make future predictions, the "unsupervised machine learning algorithms", such as "Clustering", need to be employed. For example, telecom companies often use the "clustering" technology to expand their network by identifying network tower locations with optimal signal strength in the targeted region.

Machine Learning Vs Data Science

Data science is an umbrella term that encompasses machine learning algorithms. Here are some basic distinctions between the two terms.

Data components

Data science pertains to the complete lifecycle of data and involves a variety of components including "ETL" (Extract, Transform, Load) pipeline to collect and classify data, Data visualization, distributed computing, machine learning, artificial intelligence, Data engineering, dashboards, and System deployment introduction and environment among other components. Machine learning models are provided input data and contain various components including: data separation, data exploration, problem-solving and appropriate model selection among other features.

Performance measures

Data science has no standard for performance measurement and is determined on a case-by-case basis. Typically, performance measures are an indication of Data quality, Data timeliness, Data accessibility, Data visualization capability and data query capability. Machine learning models have standard performance measures, with each algorithm having a measure to indicate the success of the model and describing the given training data set. For example, in "linear regression analysis", the "Root Mean Square Error (RME) serves as an indication error(s) in the model.

Development method

Data science project implementations are carried out in defined stages with project milestones that must be reached to fulfill set goals and targets within the constraints of time and resources. Machine learning projects are research-based and start with a hypothesis that is expected to be verified within the constraints of available data.

If you enjoyed this preview be sure to check out the full books on Amazon.com. Complete the journey and become a Python master!

Conclusion

Thank you for making it through to the end of *Python programming: An hands-on introduction to computer programming and algorithms, a project-based guide with practical exercises (Book 1)*, let's hope it was informative and able to provide you with all of the tools you need to achieve your goals whatever they may be.

The next step is to utilize your python programming skills and develop new tools and programs to solve real world problems. Python programming language has rendered itself as the language of choice for coding beginners and advanced software programmers alike. This book is written to help you master the basic concepts of Python coding and how you can utilize your coding skills to analyze a large volume of data and uncover valuable information that can otherwise be easily lost in the volume. Python was designed primarily to emphasize the readability of the programming code, and its syntax enables programmers to convey ideas using fewer lines of code. Python programming language increases the speed of operation while allowing for higher efficiency in creating system integrations. The power of programming languages in our digital world cannot be underestimated. People are increasingly reliable on the modern conveniences of smart technology and that momentum will endure for a long time. With all the instructions provided in this book, you are now ready to start developing your own innovative smart tech ideas and turn it into a major tech startup company and guide mankind towards a smarter future.

www.ingramcontent.com/pod-product-compliance
Lightning Source LLC
La Vergne TN
LVHW022306060326
832902LV00020B/3304